ŚAṄKARA SOURCE-BOOK

VOLUME III

ŚAṄKARA ON THE SOUL

ŚAṄKARA ON THE SOUL

A ŚAṄKARA SOURCE-BOOK

VOLUME III

by

A.J. ALSTON

SHANTI SADAN
LONDON

First Edition 1980
Reprinted 1985

Second Edition 2004

29 Chepstow Villas
London W11 3DR

www.shanti-sadan.org

ISBN 0-85424-057-8

Printed and bound by
J W Arrowsmith Ltd., Bristol BS3 2NT

PREFACE TO SECOND EDITION

This is the third volume of a large-scale annotated Source-Book of texts from the great Indian commentator Śaṅkara, freshly translated and arranged in systematic form under topics. The two earlier books in the series dealt with 'the Absolute' and 'the Creation'. The present book, which begins at Chapter VIII of the Source-Book as a whole, deals with 'the Soul', and completes the main exposition of Śaṅkara's theoretical doctrine. The remaining three volumes will deal with his refutation of opponents and his practical teaching.

Considered as a finite conscious being, the soul, for Śaṅkara, belongs to the realm of appearance. In its true nature, it is the infinite non-dual Consciousness that is the sole reality underlying all appearance. The grounds for so interpreting it have already been given in Volume I. The limiting factors, or 'illusory adjuncts', belong to the realm of 'name and form', described in Volume II, which itself derives from nescience. To form the appearance of an individual soul, the infinite Consciousness undergoes apparent de-limitation by the gross physical body, and also by a more permanent 'subtle body', composed of subtle matter, imperceptible to the senses. The subtle body is comprised of the sense-organs and mental faculties, and conserves the impressions of thoughts and deeds, which will prompt it, after the death of the present gross body, to don new bodies and undergo further transmigration, until the painful process is halted once and for all by 'enlightenment'.

The texts in the present volume describe the nature and functions of the bodies, gross and subtle, in which the infinite Consciousness is apparently enclosed to form the various individual souls. Two complementary analogies are used to explain the relation of the Infinite to the finite. First, the limitation of the infinite Consciousness is said to be illusory, like the illusory appearance of the 'enclosure' of infinite space in pots. And secondly, Consciousness is said to be 'reflected' in the subtle matter composing mind and sense-organs, like the sun or moon reflected in water. The individual consciousness being a mere reflection, its vicissitudes do not affect the infinite Consciousness.

The present volume contains the texts in which Śaṅkara describes the sense-organs and mental faculties, and hence it includes his theory of perception. But it does not give a complete account of his epistemology. The metaphysical bases of this have already been stated in Volume I; his texts assessing reason, authority and mystical experience (anubhava) as sources of knowledge will be given in the course of his practical teaching set out in Volumes V and VI; and some important features of his epistemological teaching come out indirectly in the course of passages in criticism of other schools to be given in Volume IV.

Śaṅkara's account of perception brings out the contrast between the activity of the sense-organs along with the mind, and the motionless stability of the light of Consciousness that illumines them. What is particularly valuable in all his theory of knowledge is the metaphysical element. He argues in Chapter IX that one must admit the existence of a pure unchanging principle of Consciousness if one is to account for the facts of experience. If consciousness persists as in some way identical through the successive states of waking, dream and dreamless sleep, then should it not be regarded as radically different in nature from the changing experiences, illumining them with its unchanging light and witnessing them as objects? Śaṅkara raises this question and answers it in the affirmative, on the basis of Vedic authority, reason and immediate experience alike. In Volume IV we shall see how, when attacking the Buddhists, he draws attention to the difficulty of accounting for recognition and memory on a purely phenomenalist or positivist basis.

PREFACE

My obligations have already been indicated in the first volume. The present one, like its predecessors, is dedicated with the deepest reverence to the late Hari Prasad Shastri, to whom the whole work owes its existence.

A. J. ALSTON

LONDON 2004

CONTENTS

page

Preface v

Sanskrit transliteration x

Chapter

VIII. The Soul and its Organs and Bodies

1. The Soul as the Self viewed under External Adjuncts 1
2. The Organs and Bodies of the Soul 26
3. The Light that Illumines the Soul 49
4. The Soul and the Lord are not Distinct 63

Notes to Chapter VIII 88

IX. The 'States' of the Soul and their Transcendence

1. Dream 103
2. Dreamless Sleep 127
3. Turīya 164

Notes to Chapter IX 197

CONTENTS

Chapter	*page*
List of General Abbreviations	211
Bibliography	214
Conspectus of the Śaṅkara Source Book	233

The General Index and the Index to Texts Cited are published at the end of Volume VI, *Śaṅkara on Enlightenment*.

TRANSLITERATED SANSKRIT WORDS

The following table gives the most elementary indications of the value of the vowels that are variable in English (but regular in Sanskrit) and of the unfamiliar symbols and groupings of letters found in transliterated Sanskrit words. It is not intended as an accurate guide to correct pronunciation, for which see M. Coulson, *Sanskrit* (Teach Yourself Books), 4-21.

a	=	u in but
ā	=	a in father
ai	=	uy as in buy
au	=	au in audit (or French au)
c	=	ch in chant
ch	=	ch aspirated (said with extra breath)
ḍ	=	d in drake
e	=	ay in hay (better, French é elongated)
h	=	immediately after a consonant aspirates it without altering the value. (bh, ph, etc.)
ḥ	=	strong h
i	=	i in hit
ī	=	ea in eat
jñ	=	ja or gya (as in big yard)
ṃ	=	m before b, p, v, y and at the end of a word; elsewhere = n
ṅ	=	n in king
ṇ	=	n in tendril
ñ	=	n (except in jñ, q.v.)
o	=	o in note
ṛ	=	ri in rich
s	=	s in such
ś	=	sh in shut
ṣ	=	sh in shut
ṭ	=	t in try
u	=	u in put
ū	=	oo in boot

CHAPTER VIII

THE SOUL AND ITS ORGANS AND BODIES

1. The Soul as the Self viewed under its Superimposed Adjuncts

In the last two chapters we have considered Śaṅkara's theory of the nature of the external world, and his arguments to show that it was not real. In the next two chapters we shall be considering his theory of the nature of the human soul, its bodies and organs and states of consciousness, and how there is a divine element in it which remains above, and untouched by, the successive states of waking, dream and dreamless sleep.

The states of consciousness of the soul and the way to their transcendence will be considered more particularly in the following chapter. The present chapter will consider the structure and make-up of the soul and how it relates to the Lord, seeing that it is in some sense evidently different from Him, while the light shining within the two is the same. The theme of the opening section is stated in its first four Extracts. The soul is the immutable Consciousness viewed in association with superimposed limiting adjuncts (upādhi),[1] and this Consciousness, appearances notwithstanding, is also present in dreamless sleep. The connection of the immutable Consciousness with superimposed adjuncts is due to nescience and can be dissolved through an awakening to an intuitive knowledge of the true nature of the Self.

Extracts 5 to 9 describe how the adjuncts in which the Self is apparently enclosed to form the multiplicity of individual souls derive from name and form as their material cause, and how the Self is in its true nature unborn and immutable, while only the adjuncts, like the gross material body, come into being and pass away.

Extracts 10 to 16 offer two alternative, or rather complementary, analogies for conceiving the relation of the Self as immutable Consciousness with its superimposed adjuncts. The immutable Consciousness is said to be reflected in its closest and most immediate adjunct, the mind with its ego-notion. Śaṅkara regarded the use of the reflection-analogy as indispensable for explaining the facts of experience, and for reconciling the fact that the experiences of each individual soul are private to himself with the presence of one Self as the reality in all. Another useful analogy for explaining the apparent individuation of the Self as the multiplicity of individual souls is that of the apparent separation of individual parcels of the ether of space within various pots. The latter analogy has the advantage of showing that liberation, which corresponds to the 'release' of space through the destruction of the pot, consists in simple identity with the Absolute, and not in any form of 'association' (sāyujya) with the supreme deity, however close.[2] The reflection-analogy, which is much the more important for Śaṅkara, as later sections will show, has the incidental advantage of suggesting to the beginner on the practical path that, even if he cannot attain to the Absolute at a single leap, he can acquire a higher degree of awareness of the presence of the Absolute in the course of daily life through purification of the mind, the medium in which its light is reflected.[3] The final Extract (No.17) argues that the texts in the Upanishads speaking of the soul as 'minute' are not meant to characterize it in its true nature, but refer to it as it appears under superimposed adjuncts. On this head, Śaṅkara's interpretation of the all-important text, Brahma Sūtra II.iii.29 'tad-guṇa-sāratvāt tu tad-vyapadeśaḥ prājñavat' conflicts with that of the theistic Vedanta of the sectarian schools[4] and with the interpretation more usually offered by modern scholars.[5] Śaṅkara's supporting arguments make rather tedious reading, being highly theological in character, and are perhaps not of much importance for understanding his general philosophical doctrine. Accordingly, only one short passage has been here selected, in which he states his main position briefly and dogmatically.

TEXTS ON THE SOUL AS THE SELF VIEWED UNDER ITS SUPERIMPOSED ADJUNCTS

1. The Absolute, transcendent, beyond modification, assumes the appearance of the individual soul through the influence of (superimposed) external adjuncts (upādhi). For the traditional Vedic teaching is that Consciousness is the very nature of the Absolute, as in such texts as... 'Entirely a mass of Consciousness, having nothing inside it and nothing outside it'.[6] If the individual soul is nothing other than the transcendent Absolute mentioned in these texts, then we must conclude that the soul, too, must have eternal and immutable Consciousness for its very nature, as fire has heat and light....

Nor does it follow that if the Self be eternal and immutable Consciousness by nature, organs such as the sense of smell are useless, as their function is to focus consciousness onto particular objects like odours. For, as the Upanishad text in question says, 'The nose is for smelling'.[7]

Again, it has been held that those who are (unaware of their surroundings) in dreamless sleep, and in fainting, coma or trance, are not conscious, (and consequently that consciousness comes and goes and is not the true nature of the soul). But this view is refuted by the Vedic texts themselves, as in such passages about a sleeping person as 'Verily, when there (in the state of dreamless sleep) he does not see, he is, indeed, seeing though he does not see, for there is no cessation of the seeing of the seer, because the latter is imperishable. There is not then, however, a second thing apart from himself that he could see'.[8] The point is that the appearance of not being conscious that characterizes these states (of dreamless sleep, etc.) arises from the absence of any objects to be conscious of, not from the absence of consciousness. It is like the light pervading the empty space between solid objects, which is imperceptible, not because it is not present but because there is nothing for it to illuminate.[9]

❖

2. Now, this connection of the soul with the (superimposed) external adjunct of intellect is invariably associated with nescience (false knowledge), and nescience cannot come to an end except through right knowledge. As long, therefore, as there is no awakening to one's own Self as the Absolute, so long connection with the adjunct called intellect continuously persists. And a Vedic text, too, points this out in the words, 'I know this great Spirit, beyond darkness (nescience), of the brilliance of the sun. It is only through knowing Him that one goes beyond death. There is no other path for the attainment of the final goal'.[10]

It might be thought impossible to believe in the connection of the soul with the intellect during dreamless sleep and in periods of world-dissolution. For we have the text, 'Then, my dear one, he attains the goal, he departs to his own Self'.[11] And it is admitted that in that state (of dreamless sleep) all modifications are dissolved. So how can one maintain that connection with the intellect persists *continuously* as long as the soul remains in transmigratory life?

To this the author of the Sūtras replies: 'But (this connection with the intellect) continues to exist potentially, like virility, etc., because it retains the power to manifest'. We see in the world that, in childhood and certain other states, virility and other qualities are not perceived, while in manhood and so forth they become manifest. And it cannot be that in manhood they suddenly emerge from non-existence, or we would find them suddenly emerging in the case of eunuchs and the like. In the same way, this connection of the soul with the intellect that we are discussing exists in potential form during periods of dreamless sleep and world-dissolution, and then manifests again at the time of awakening or of creation at the beginning of a new world-period. And this is the only possible explanation of the matter. For nothing can come into being fortuitously (uncaused), or, if it could, one might as well admit that anything could come out of anything. And the Veda itself shows that awakening from dreamless sleep is caused by the presence of a seed of nescience, in such texts as, 'Though they have attained to the Real (in dreamless sleep), they are not conscious that they have attained to the Real'....[12] So it stands proved that connection with the intellect persists continuously as long as the soul remains in transmigratory life.[13]

❖

3. Well, why not take the complex of the Vital Energy and the body itself for the experiencer? What is the point of assuming any experiencer beyond these?

It is not right to speak thus. For a difference was seen to have been introduced by the pushing (of the sleeping man by Ajātaśatru). If the experiencer were simply the complex of the Vital Energy and the body, there would be no difference, as regards awakening, between a sleeper who was pushed and a sleeper who was not. But if there was a sleeper over and above the complex of the Vital Energy and the body and separate from it, then the difference becomes intelligible. For such an experiencer could well undergo the different sensations of being left alone and being pushed, because his past relations with the complex of the Vital Energy and the body would have been many and various, and because he could be expected to undergo fluctuations of fortune as a result of his past deeds, good, bad and indifferent, leading to various degrees of pleasure, pain and delusion.[14] But in the case of the mere complex of the Vital Energy and the body, no changes could arise as a result of past deeds or past relations with other entities. Nor would the degree of loudness of voice or roughness of touch affect the matter in the slightest. But they do in fact do so, because, when the sleeping man did not wake up at a light touch, Ajātaśatru was able to wake him by repeatedly shaking him with his hand. Thus that one who was awoken by the shaking, who seemed to be flaming and flashing with fire and to have been summoned from somewhere else, and who quite transfigured the body by conferring on it various forms of consciousness and activity, must have been other than the body.[15]

4. And there (in the body) he has (as the Upanishad states) 'three abodes'. During the hours of waking he occupies the place of the organ of vision in the right eye; during dream he occupies the inner organ, the mind; and in dreamless sleep he dwells in the ether of the heart....

Here, in these three abodes, the Lord, who has entered into the body as the soul, experiences these dreams called waking, dream and dreamless sleep. Even the waking state is a kind of dream, because there is no awakening to one's own Self as the supreme reality, and because one sees unreal objects as in dream....

The soul exists in these three abodes alternately, identifying himself with them through natural nescience, afflicted for ages with an overpowering sleep from which he does not awake even under the hammer-like blows of many hundreds of thousands of painful disasters.[16]

❖

5. Becoming progressively grosser in nature as they undergo further manifestation, name and form (having manifested originally as the name and form of the ether) first become of the nature of the wind. From wind they become fire, from fire water, from water earth. In this way, with each previous state of name and form passing over into the next in a definite order, the great elements (mahā-bhūta) are produced, ending with earth. Thus the earth is penetrated by all the five great elements.

And from the earth spring rice, barley and other crops, all partaking of the five elements.[17] From these, when eaten, arise the blood and seed that pertain to the body of woman and man respectively. At the time of union, friction arises from the agitations of lust — which stems from ignorance — and this friction draws forth blood and seed which are deposited in the womb and consecrated by a mantram. Juices from the womb enter this unit of blood and seed, and it grows and becomes an embryo and is eventually born in the ninth or tenth month.

Once born, it acquires a name and form and receives further consecration at the Jātakarman and other ceremonies.[18] Then, later, it undergoes the Upanayana consecration and becomes known as a student of the sacred texts (brahmacārin).[19] That body, united with a wife through a ceremony of consecration, becomes a householder. That very same, through consecration as a forest-dweller (vāna-prastha), becomes known as an ascetic (tāpasa). And that very same, through a ceremony bringing all ritualistic action to an end, becomes known as a houseless wandering monk (parivrāj). And thus the body, conditioned by birth, parentage and consecration, is different from you (who are self-existent and so not conditioned in your true essence).

And the mind and senses, also, are of the nature of name and form only, as is known from such upanishadic texts as 'For the mind is composed of food, my dear one'.

And if you are wondering, 'How am I void of distinct caste, parentage and consecration?', then listen. He who brings name and form into manifestation is Himself different from name and form. He it is who, manifesting name and form, having projected this body, though Himself without consecration or any other empirical characteristics, enters name and form, who Himself sees, though not seen by others, who hears, though He is not heard, who knows but cannot be known.[20]

❖

6. It might be that someone would fall into the error of supposing that the individual soul, too, (i.e. as well as the cosmic elements and the organism and its cognitive and active powers which are rooted in them) might be subject to origination and dissolution. For we speak ordinarily of Devadatta as 'having been born' or as 'having died', and moreover ceremonies such as the Jātakarman have been laid down to mark and consecrate these events. If anyone does have this erroneous notion, however, we propose to dispel it. There can be no origination or dissolution of the soul if it is to be connected with the future fruits of its deeds as laid down in the Veda. If the soul came to an end with the body, the injunctions and prohibitions of the Veda concerned with obtaining desirable results and avoiding undesirable ones in a future birth would be meaningless. And the Veda actually says, 'Verily, this body dies when deprived of the soul, whereas the soul does not die'.[21]

But has it not been said that we speak in the world of the birth and death of the individual soul (jīva)? Certainly it has been said. But this reference to the soul as being subject to birth and death is figurative.... The Sūtra affirms, 'The reference is to fixed and moving bodies'.... These are what are born and die, and the words 'birth' and 'death' apply to them in the primary sense. And they are applied metaphorically to the soul inhabiting these bodies, because, as the Sūtra puts it,

'It is only when there is a body that there is birth and death'. The terms 'birth' and 'death', indeed, can only be applied when a body arises or disappears, and not otherwise. No one sees an individual soul (jīva) to be born or to die except in association with a body. 'Verily this person, when he is born and obtains a body, (becomes connected with evils). When he departs on dying (he leaves all evils behind)'.[22] This text shows how the words 'birth' and 'death' refer (not to the origination or destruction of the soul but) to the connection of the soul with, or its severence from, the body.[23]

❖

7. Well, but was it not said that the soul must be a modification because it is composite, and that because it is a modification it must come into being (and have a beginning)? To this we reply as follows: The fact of the soul's being composite does not proceed from its own intrinsic nature, for we have the text 'The one divine principle stands hidden in all beings, all-pervading, the inmost Self of all creatures'.[24] Its appearance of being composite is occasioned through external adjuncts, such as the lower and higher aspects of the mind, the senses and the body, just as relation with external adjuncts like pots occasions the appearance of divisions in the ether (or space). And the Veda itself declares that it is the one Absolute, beyond modification, that becomes involved with the plurality of reason and the other faculties, in such passages as 'Verily, this Self which becomes identified with the higher mind (buddhi), identified with the lower mind (manas) identified with sight, identified with hearing, is the Absolute'.[25] Its 'being identified' expresses not its own true nature but its nature as coloured by that with which it is

identified, as when we say 'That wretched fellow is nothing but women!'

It is true that we occasionally hear of the 'origination' and 'dissolution' of the soul in the Veda, but this has to be understood to refer to its coming into association with or severance from adjuncts (in particular with the physical body). The soul's 'origination' is through the origination of the adjunct and its 'dissolution' through the dissolution of the adjunct. The words 'Venerable master, you have brought me to the utmost confusion. Verily, I cannot understand "There is no consciousness after death"' are followed by the answer, 'Lo, I say nothing that could be a source of confusion. This Self is verily indestructible. But there comes a time when it parts company with the organs that make empirical experience possible'.[26] And the purport intended to be conveyed in the topic (namely, that the individual soul does not originate and dissolve like the ether and other elements) is not contradicted, as the soul is taken to be none other than the Absolute, which is beyond modification, while the fact that the Absolute and the soul also possess distinct characteristics is set down as due to the external limiting adjuncts associated with the soul (which, as external, do not affect its intrinsic nature).[27]

❖

8. If the Absolute is one without a second from the standpoint of final truth, pure and untouched by the pains of transmigratory life, then whence comes this lump-like form of the Self,[28] overlaid by such features of transmigratory experience as 'born', 'dead', 'happy', 'miserable', 'I' and 'mine'?

We reply: The words in the Upanishad text 'From these elements' refer to the body and sense-organs of the individual soul and the objects it enjoys, which evolve from those elements. These factors in the life of the individual are of the nature of name and form and are comparable to the foam and bubbles, where the supreme Self stands as the pure water. It has already been declared that all this, down to the objects of the senses, dissolves into the Absolute as massed Consciousness (prajñāna-ghana) like rivers into the sea through a knowledge of the final truth attained through discrimination.

'From these elements' — that is, from the body, sense-organs and objects — designated as (empirical) reality (satya), the soul arises 'like a lump of salt'. As a reflection of the sun or moon comes up on water, or as red colour comes up on a crystal from some object dyed red and placed near it so as to constitute its 'external adjunct', so the Self arises as a 'lump' in the form of the individual soul, formed through the (super-imposed) external adjuncts of the body, mind and senses. Eventually the elements as transformed into the individual organism and the objects of its experience — which are what condition the lump-like form of the individual soul — are dissolved like rivers in the sea through the instructions of the Veda and the Teacher. When they vanish like foam and bubbles on the water, this lump-like individual existence vanishes with them. When the reflection of the sun or moon in the water, or the reflection of colour in the crystal, is destroyed by the removal of one of the factors of the reflection, be it the water in which the luminaries are reflected or the object dyed red which is reflected in the crystal, then the moon, the sun or the crystal stand out in their true nature. And in the same way, with the removal of the individual consciousness, massed Consciousness stands out in its true nature, infinite, unfathomable, pure and bright.[29]

❖

9. Thus addressed, the pupil replied: If I were nothing more than the psycho-physical complex, then I could not perform the mutual superimposition of body and Self, because I would be non-conscious, and would exist for the sake of another. But if I were to conclude from this that I must be the Self, transcendent, other than the psycho-physical complex, existent for my own sake because conscious, then superimposition, the seed of all evil, would have been deliberately performed by myself on myself (which is absurd).

Thus addressed, the Teacher replied: If you think that erroneous superimposition is the seed of all evil, then do not do it.

Sir, I cannot prevent myself. I am prompted to it by something else (other than myself) and am not free in the matter.

Then in that case, since (being on your own admission a passive instrument) you are not a conscious being, you cannot exist for your own sake. That by whose prompting you act unfreely must be conscious and exist for itself. You must be just the (*per se*) non-conscious psycho-physical complex (which it uses as an instrument).

If I am non-conscious, how is it that I experience pleasure and pain, and understand what you say to me?

The Teacher said: Are you different from the feelings of pleasure and pain and from what I say to you, or are you non-different?

The pupil said: Well, I am not non-different. For I know both of them as objects, like a pot. If I were non-different from either of them, then I could not know them. But I do in fact know them. Therefore I am different from them. And if I were not different from them, those transient modes, the feelings of pleasure and pain (would not be mere objects of my experience but) would exist for their own sake, and so would what you have said to me. But it is not reasonable to hold that they could exist for their own sake. For the pleasure occasioned by sandalwood and the pain occasioned by thorns do not exist for the benefit of the sandalwood and the thorns. Nor does the use of a pot exist for the benefit of the pot. Therefore sandalwood and the like exist for my sake, the one who experiences them. For I am the one who knows everything that comes into my mind, and am myself different from it.

The Teacher said to him: Then, evidently, you exist for your own sake, because you are conscious and are not prompted to act by another. No one who is conscious is unfree and prompted to act by another, for one conscious being cannot exist for the sake of another, since both are identical, like the light of two lamps. Nor can that which has consciousness serve the ends of that which does not have consciousness, because the latter, from the very fact of being without consciousness, has no ends of its own to pursue. Nor do we find two non-conscious things serving each other's ends mutually. The beam and the wall do not serve each other's purposes mutually.[30]

But is it not a fact that two conscious beings, master and servant, though equal in point of being conscious, are seen to serve each other's ends mutually?

That is beside the point.[31] For I meant to speak of you as conscious in the sense that fire has heat and light,[32] and I gave the example of the light of the two lamps. This being so, you experience everything that enters into your mind through your eternal and ever-changeless consciousness, comparable to the heat and light of the fire. If, then, you agree that your Self is ever void of distinctions in this way, why did you ask, 'After repeatedly attaining respite in dreamless sleep, I again experience pain in waking and dream. Is this my very nature or is it something adventitious?' Has that delusion gone or not?

Thus addressed, the pupil replied: Sir, that delusion has gone by your grace.[33]

❖

10. *Objection:* It is not reasonable to suppose that this omniscient Deity, Himself independent and not subject to transmigratory experience, should deliberately enter the body, associated as it is with a thousand evils, and should identify Himself with it with the idea 'Let me experience pain'.

Answer: True enough, it would not have been reasonable if He had decided to enter into the elements with His own true form and willed to experience pain. But He did not enter into them in this way. How did He enter into them, then? As this individual soul (jīva). The individual soul is a mere reflection (ābhāsa)[34] of the Deity.

A reflection (pratibimba) of the Spirit (puruṣa) enters, as it were, into the 'mirror' arising from its own contact with the intellect and, through that, with the elements. The process is like the reflection of the sun and other luminous bodies 'entering' into water and other reflecting media. This contact of the Deity of infinite and unthinkable power with the intellect and the rest constitutes a reflection of consciousness arising from a failure to discriminate the true nature of the Deity, and it gives rise to a variety of false notions such as 'I am happy', 'I am miserable' and 'I am bewildered'.[35] Because the Deity only enters as the individual soul, as a mere reflection, it is not itself in any way connected with bodily characteristics such as pleasure and pain. Men and the sun, when they 'enter' mirrors or water as reflections, are not themselves really connected with reflecting media, and the same is true of the Deity...

Objection: If the individual soul is a mere reflection, it must be unreal. In that case, how can one defend the statements in the Veda saying that it sojourns in this world and also in the next?

Answer: There is nothing wrong here, as we hold that it is real (when considered) as the real Self. The whole mass of modifications consisting of name and form, etc., are illusory considered in themselves, but real as the Self. For it is said in the Veda, 'A modification is the object of a name, a mere suggestion of speech'. This holds for the individual soul as well.[36]

❖

11. The next form of the Self is that in which it has 'entered' (into the elements) as enjoyer and agent, like the sun

'entering' (through its reflection) into water or some other reflecting medium. He is (the text says) the seer, the one who touches, the hearer, the one who smells, the one who tastes, the thinker, the understander, the agent, of the nature of consciousness. When the term 'consciousness' (vijñāna) is understood as that through which one is conscious, it means the instruments of cognition such as the intellect, etc. But here consciousness means the agent in the act of knowing, the one who knows. 'Of the nature of consciousness' means the one whose nature is to be the agent in the act of knowing.[37] He is called the Spirit (puruṣa) inasmuch as He fills (pūrṇa) the delimiting adjunct (upādhi) consisting of the aggregate of physical and psychical instruments (forming the individual person).

And just as the reflection of the sun in water or some other reflecting medium returns to the sun (on the destruction of the reflecting medium), so does the agent 'of the nature of consciousness' find its goal in the supreme Self, the Immutable, that which remains over as the ultimate support of the universe.[38]

❖

12. The reflection (ābhāsa) of the face is different from the face, since it conforms to (some of the characteristics of) the mirror; the face is different from the reflection, because it does not conform to the mirror. We hold that the reflection of the Self in the (mind in the form of) ego-sense is comparable to the reflection of the face, while the Self is comparable to the face and therefore different from the reflection. And yet in ordinary empirical experience the two remain undifferentiated....

Some say that the bare reflection (ābhāsa), the ego-sense, is itself the transmigrating entity. A reflection, they say, is a reality, as we know from the authority of the Dharma Śāstras[39] and also because it causes real results such as coolness....

(We reply that, as we have already established,) the reflection of the face in the mirror is a property neither of the mirror nor the face. If it were a property of either of them, it would persist in one or other of them when the two were parted. It might be thought that because one speaks of the reflection of the face as 'the face' it must be a property of the face. But this is wrong. For on the one hand the reflection conforms to certain characteristics of the mirror (which would not be possible if it were a property of the face). And on the other hand it ceases to manifest when the face is still in existence (but parted from the mirror, so that it cannot be a property of the mirror). If you say that it is a property of both the mirror and the face when they are in conjunction, that also is wrong, as it is not invariably perceived when they are both present in conjunction (but inappropriately placed).

Then you may say that seeing the reflection is seeing a second independent real entity which, in itself invisible, becomes visible in some other entity, as Rāhu becomes visible in the sun and moon. But the reality of Rāhu is established in advance by the Veda.[40] And if Rāhu be taken as a shadow,[41] then it must be an unreality according to our previous reasoning. As for the text prohibiting the stepping over the shadow of certain persons (quoted from Smṛti), its purpose is merely to prohibit an act. It cannot establish the reality (or unreality) of anything. A sentence having a given purpose cannot have quite a different purpose at the same time.[42] The delight of coolness (proceeding from shadows, mentioned as a proof of their substantial existence), too, proceeds from the absence of anything hot. When the delight of coolness has a positive cause, the latter is perceptible, as in the case of water. But shade is not perceptible as anything positive.

Thus the Veda and reason point to a Self, a reflection (ābhāsa) of that Self, and a receptacle for that reflection, on the analogy of the face, its reflection and the receptacle for that reflection (the mirror). They also point to the unreality of the reflection.

To whom, then, belongs the property of being the transmigrant? Not to pure Consciousness, for it is not subject to modification. Not to the reflection, for that is not a reality. And not to the ego-sense (the receptacle of the reflection) since it is *per se* non-conscious. Transmigration, therefore, must be mere nescience (avidyā) arising from non-discrimination. It only possesses being and appears to afflict the Self on account of the (presence behind it of that) changeless Self. Just as the rope-snake, though unreal, possesses being by virtue of the rope, until it is discriminated from it, so also does the complex of Self, receptacle and reflection possess being by virtue of the changeless Self, until it is discriminated from it.

Some say that it is the ego (understood as the soul, self-existent but individual) that undergoes modification through its own cognitions, and that it is the ego which is ever-existent and which experiences pleasure, pain and transmigration.[43] These persons, bereft of the true Vedic tradition, are deluded through lack of a right knowledge of the

Self and its reflection, and so come to identify the true Self with the ego-sense. For them transmigratory experience in the form of agency and enjoyerhood is a *reality*. Because they do not perform discrimination, they do not know (i.e. do not analyse the true nature of empirical experience and discover) the existence of the Self, its reflection and the receptacle of the reflection. And so they continue to experience transmigration. But if, on the other hand, it be accepted that the intellect is illumined by a reflection of that Consciousness whose real nature is the Self, then it also becomes intelligible how the Veda can refer (indirectly) to the Self by words meaning knowledge.[44]

❖

13. Teaching can be significant only if addressed to a hearer. And if, as we are agreed, the Witness is not the (active) hearer, who else could be the hearer? If you (the Sāṅkhya philosopher) say that the intellect could be the hearer in virtue of its (mere) proximity to the Witness, this is wrong. For the Witness can, as such,[45] be of no more help to the intellect in hearing than a block of wood. And even if the Witness did in some way help the intellect to know, would not that imply the unacceptable consequence that it acted and so underwent modification?[46] But if a reflection is admitted, this difficulty does not arise. And the reflection hypothesis is moreover supported by the Veda[47] and other traditional sources.[48]

And if you say that the hypothesis of a reflection itself implies the modification of the reflected entity, that is wrong, for it is like the appearance of a snake in a rope and illusions of that kind, and like the reflection of a face in a mirror, as we said. You may say that no reflection of the Self is perceived independently of the Self, while the face and the mirror are apprehended independently of one another, so that the reflection of the Self can only be established by circular reasoning.[49] For we require to know that the Self exists independently of the reflection before we can say that the reflection is in fact a reflection of the Self. And we require to know that the reflection is in fact a reflection of the Self before we can say that the Self exists independently of it.

But this is not so. For in dream, the mental modifications beheld by the Witness are known to be distinct from it. In that state there are no external chariots, etc., so that there must be direct apprehension of mental modifications by the Self.[50]

❖

14. Furthermore, the individual soul is, as the author of the Sūtra puts it, 'a mere reflection' of the supreme Self. It has to be taken as a reflection of the supreme Self like a reflection of the sun in water. The individual soul is not to be identified with the supreme Self flatly. And yet it is not a separate reality. And just as the other reflections of the sun in other water-surfaces do not all necessarily undergo a tremor when one of them does, so, when one individual soul becomes connected with the reward of any piece of work, it does not follow that all the others do too. So there is no confusion, either in regard to action or to the rewards of action (arising from the fact that the Self in all individual souls is ultimately one). And because a reflection is a product of nescience, it is intelligible that the transmigratory life that rests on it should also be a product of nescience. Hence it is also intelligible that the true nature of the Self should be taught to be the Absolute through the elimination of nescience.[51]

15. A part of Myself, the supreme Self, Nārāyaṇa, becomes the eternal soul in the world of transmigratory experience, the well-known 'agent and enjoyer'.

The reflected image of the sun in water, which is a part[52] of the sun, goes back to the sun when the reflecting medium is removed, and never again comes forth. And this soul, as part of the Self, goes back to the Self in the same way. Similarly, the part of external space apparently enclosed within its external adjunct (upādhi), the pot, being a 'part' of the universal ether or space in general, dissolves into the latter on the destruction of its adjunct and never re-emerges. So the Lord's words 'My supreme abode, having attained which no one returns', were quite justifiable and intelligible.

But what can it mean to say that the supreme Self, which is partless, has parts or pieces? If it were composed of parts, indeed, it would undergo destruction, and the parts would eventually disintegrate.[53] But there is nothing wrong here. For the meaning is that the part is marked off by external adjuncts set up by nescience. The soul is therefore only imagined as a part. It is 'as if' a part.[54]

❖

16. The supreme Self, because it is imperceptible, partless and all-pervading like the ether, is described in the Veda as *like* the ether. And this supreme Self, said to be like the ether, is spoken of as constituting the individual souls in the same way that the ether undergoes 'production' in the form of (apparent) isolated portions of ether 'enclosed' within pots. That is to say, when we hear in the Upanishads of the rise of the individual souls from the supreme Self, that has to be

understood in the same sense that 'units' of ether are said to 'arise' in pots, (apparently carved out) from the great cosmic ether. It has not to be taken as an actual fact.

Just as composite objects like pots themselves ultimately arise from the ether,[55] similarly all objects composed of the elements, as well as the organs and instruments of the individual organism, arise from the supreme Self in the same way, imagined like a snake erroneously perceived in a rope. Hence the text says that the Self 'is born' through organisms, like the separate portions of ether 'undergoing production' in pots.

The Teacher's (i.e. Gauḍapāda's) meaning is that when the Veda, solely with a view to instruct the dull-witted student, speaks of the 'birth' of the Self, then 'the birth' of the Self in the form of the individual soul has to be understood as analogous to the 'production' of isolated portions of ether within pots.

The isolated portions of ether are 'produced' by the production of the pots and the like. And the same portions of ether 'dissolve' into the great cosmic ether with the destruction of the pots. In the same way, the individual soul undergoes 'birth' through the rise of the physical organism and 'dissolves' back into the Self with the dissolution of this.[56] It is not that the soul undergoes either birth or dissolution at all in its own intrinsic nature (which is pure Consciousness).[57]

❖

17. The notion that the soul is minute is wrong. We have already explained how the individual soul is none other than

the Absolute, because the Veda does not speak of it as having an origin, and teaches that it is in fact the Absolute itself that 'enters' into the world as the soul, and that the Absolute and the soul are identical. If the soul is none other than the Absolute, then the soul must extend as far as the Absolute extends. And the Absolute is declared in the Veda to be all-pervading, so that the soul must be all-pervading too. Moreover, the all-pervasiveness of the soul is championed specifically in many of the texts of the Veda and Smṛti, as for instance in the text 'That great unborn Self which is identified with reason and lies in the midst of the organs'.[58] Nor could the soul really have direct perception of the whole body if it were minute. And it will not do to say that it could do so through its contact with the sense of touch (which lies spread over the surface of the body), for this would imply that a prick from a thorn would be felt over the whole body (and not only localized in one place). For the contact between the thorn and the general sense of touch (located in the skin) would be generalized through the whole extent of the sense of touch, which in turn pervades the whole body. But the fact is that one who treads on a thorn feels the pain in the sole of his foot only.

Nor can what is minute pervade anything else through one of its qualities. For a quality has the same location as the substance in which it inheres. If a quality did not inhere in its substance it would cease to be its quality (and become an independent substance). The fact that the light of a lamp is another substance separate from the lamp has already been explained. Assuming that an odour is also a quality, it can travel about only as accompanied by its own substratum (some microscopic particle from the fragrant substance), otherwise it would cease to be a quality. And in this vein Dvaipāyana (Vyāsa) has said, 'Some unintelligent people, having perceived an odour in water, have declared that it inhered in that substance. But one should know that it inheres ever in (particles of) earth, though it mingles with water and wind'.[59]

Moreover, if the consciousness of the soul pervades the whole body, it follows from this very fact that the soul cannot be minute. For consciousness is the very nature of the soul, as heat and light are the very nature of fire: it is not that we have to think of a distinct substance and quality here. And since the notion that the soul is of the same size as the body has already been refuted (in dealing with the doctrines of the Jainas),[60] the soul must be all-pervading, as that is the only remaining possibility.

If you ask why, when the soul is all-pervading, it is referred to in the Veda as minute, the author of the Sūtras replies, 'The soul is spoken of in this way because in it the qualities of that (the intellect) appear to predominate'. The qualities of the intellect (buddhi) are desire and aversion, joy and sorrow, etc. When these appear to predominate in the soul it is fit for transmigratory life. Its very nature as the individual soul is to have the qualities of the intellect appearing to predominate in it. The Self in its own true nature as isolated from the qualities of the intellect does not have these qualities and does not undergo transmigration. The 'being an agent' and the 'being an experiencer' of the supreme Self, which is by nature ever free and not an agent or an enjoyer or subject to transmigration, arises from the erroneous superimposition onto it of the characteristics of the intellect and other external adjuncts.

Therefore, when the qualities of the intellect appear to predominate in the soul, the dimensions of the intellect are spoken of in the Veda as being the dimensions of the soul. And when the soul is said to 'withdraw' (from the physical body at death, and transmigrate to other bodies), such activities pertain to the soul only through the organs with which it has been identified. This withdrawal (and transmigration) do not pertain to the soul in its own inner nature.[61]

2. The Organs and Bodies of the Soul

We have seen[62] that the physical body of the soul is firmly anchored in the earth-element, as the earth consumed in the form of food by the parents is transmuted in their bodies into the form of blood and seed, the elements contributed respectively by the mother and father, from which the child develops. The earth-element itself is the final and grossest product of a process of emanation of the elements that begins with the ether and becomes progressively more determinate and less pervasive as each element in the series emanates from the preceding one. Earth (and hence food, which grows from the earth,) contains all the qualities of all the five elements in gross or manifest form.

The physical body, however, is only the passing, external frame or receptacle for the soul. The latter has another closer-fitting and longer-lasting 'seventeen-fold' body consisting of the five senses (hearing, touch, sight, taste and smell), the five powers of activity (handling, walking, speaking, excretion and generation), the five Vital Functions that animate and energize the physical body from within, and the mind in its two aspects, higher and lower. This more intimate vesture of the soul outlasts all physical bodies and transmigrates from one to another, containing the life, Vital Energy and intelligence that sustains and illumines each. It is supported by the subtle impressions left by the acts and thoughts of the individual soul, which keep it in being as it progresses from one body to the next until it is finally dissolved by the act of spiritual 'discrimination' which brings liberation. This doctrine is not to be found fully-formed in the classical Upanishads, but was elaborated by the Sāṅkhya philosophers. Long before Śaṅkara's day, it had become part of traditional belief amongst those who, like him, paid respect to the Smṛti as well as the Veda.

From the Brahma Sūtras, however, which also accepted the Smṛti as authoritative, Śaṅkara derived a special theory, of Vedic origins and not found in the Sāṅkhya works, according to which the soul constructs for itself a special body for the after-life on the moon, which arises from material offered in ritualistic sacrifices.[63] But for Śaṅkara this body, too, is but an external shell which becomes exhausted, while the more intimate body persists and returns to the earth for more experience in accordance with a part of its past acts and desires.

Śaṅkara calls this more intimate body the Liṅga Śarīra. 'Liṅga' means a sign by which the presence of something is inferred, for example the smoke by which one infers the existence of an unperceived entity, namely the fire hidden behind the mountain. The Liṅga Śarīra, therefore, for Śaṅkara is the body whose existence can only be inferred. He calls it 'subtle' (sūkṣma) because it is imperceptible by bystanders when it slips out of the physical body at death,[64] but he does not actually refer to it by the technical term 'Subtle Body' (sūkṣma-śarīra), though this was already current in his day. He says very little about it, and even less about the 'Causal Body'. The latter concept, which he seems to identify flatly with nescience, is only once mentioned in the whole range of his probably authentic works, and was clearly of no great importance to him. It was not the Causal Body but the Liṅga Śarīra, both in its individual and cosmic forms, that he regarded as the repository of the impressions of past acts, desires and experiences.[65] In some texts he speaks of 'Prājña' as the Universal Consciousness associated with the totality of nescience in its unmanifest or seed form, from which all limited manifestations, including Brahmā or Hiraṇyagarbha, might be said to spring.

Extracts 1 to 6 below will explain how each of the senses is composed of the same material element that it perceives,[66] and how experience indicates that a further organ must exist beyond the senses to co-ordinate their activities. This organ (mind or intellect) has four different modes, buddhi, manas, citta and ahaṅkāra, but Śaṅkara does not say much about them or consistently distinguish them. Śaṅkara's main aim in his analysis of cognition was to concentrate attention on the luminous element in it, as the following section will show, and it may be that he thought that any exact or detailed analysis of the actual mechanism of the mind, the mere instrument of cognition, external relative to the inner light that illumines it, would have distracted attention from the main subject in hand.[67] The term 'buddhi' has been translated 'intellect' according to convention, but it includes will as well as cognition.

Extracts 7 to 10 will describe the functioning of the Vital Energies in the body, and explain how they are not private to the individual, but modifications of one great force, presided over by different subordinate deities.

Extract 11 will describe the five 'selves' or 'sheaths' mentioned in the Taittirīya Upanishad. In practical life, the soul naturally identifies itself with the physical body. But reflection soon shows that there must also be a principle of Vital Energy present in the body which is different from the latter and on which the body greatly depends for its active and cognitive powers. Total identification with the mere physical body is thus exposed as an error. But the Vital Principle is in turn exposed as a mere instrument of something higher, as also are mind, knowledge and the principle of bliss successively. At last the mind is led to see that all empirically knowable aspects of the personality have to be rejected as not-self in favour of that transcendent Self for whose sake they exist. Indeed, it is only from the standpoint of nescience that they exist at all, and Śaṅkara's pupil Sureśvara declares that the whole doctrine of the five 'sheaths' (kośa) is introduced not to affirm that the Self is really surrounded by five sheaths, like so many cocoons, but as a mere device to help the student realize that all the empirical elements in his personality are impermanent and unreal.[68] Both in his Brahma Sūtra Commentary (I.i.12) and in his Taittirīya Commentary, Śaṅkara criticizes the view of earlier commentators that the bliss-self should be identified with the Absolute.[69]

Extracts 12 and 13 describe the Liṅga Śarīra. The one text in which the term Kāraṇa Śarīra (causal body) occurs, is given at Extract 14. Extracts 15 and 16 trace all connections with powers and faculties to nescience.

TEXTS ON THE ORGANS AND BODIES OF THE SOUL

1. Why is it that in all cases (of describing the dissolution of the elements at the time of the Cosmic Dissolution) the dissolution of the elements is mentioned, but not that of the sense-organs which apprehend them? It is true that this is so. But the Veda teaches that each sense-organ is composed of the same element as that which it apprehends, and not of a different one. The sense-organ is but a particular form or condition (saṃsthāna) of the great element that is the object of its own perception. It is the form or condition in which that element is adapted to apprehend itself. Just as a lamp, which

is a particular concentration of (light in the form of) colour, is an instrument for illumining all colours, so are the sense-organs special forms (of the various great elements) adapted to illumining their own particular element wherever it is found in objects. Therefore there was no need to trouble to mention the dissolution of the sense-organs separately. For since they are composed of the same universals as their objects, it is clear that they must become dissolved when the objects are dissolved.[70]

❖

2. Out of these (mind, speech and Vital Energy), a doubt presents itself initially as to the existence and nature of the mind. In reply to it the text answers that a mind (manas) must exist over and above the external sense-organs like the ears, etc. For it is a familiar experience to find that a person does not apprehend an object even though his out-going sense-organs are in contact with it and also with his soul within, and the object is nearby and in front of him. When asked if he saw such and such a colour he replies, 'My mind was elsewhere. I was absent-minded. I did not see it'. Or if someone says to him, 'Did you hear what I said?' he will say, 'My mind was elsewhere. I did not hear it. I was not listening'. Hence it follows that, even when the eye and other organs are in contact with colours and other objects of sense-experience, there is another faculty in play over and above the senses, in the 'absence' (or distraction) of which such objects are not known, and in the 'presence' (or attention) of which they are known. And this other faculty is the mind (manas) or inner organ (antaḥ-karaṇa), which takes all the sense-organs for its object. Thus the whole world sees, in the last resort, through

the mind and hears through the mind, since there is no sight or hearing when the mind is 'absent'....

And a further reason why the mind must exist is given, a further reason why there must be an inner organ called mind. When one is touched on the back in an area of the body where one cannot see, one is yet able to make distinctions and say 'That was a touch of someone's hand' or 'That was a touch of someone's knee'. How could this distinction be made by the mere skin (sense of touch) if there was no mind as discriminating faculty over and above it? The cause of such discriminative knowledge is the mind.[71]

❖

3. There are five different kinds of cognition, having sound, touch, colour, taste and odour for their objects, and five different sense-organs which effect the five different kinds of cognition. And there are five different kinds of bodily activity, namely talking (tongue), accepting (hands), moving about (feet), excretion and procreation, effected by the five different organs of activity. And over and above these (for the eleventh) there is the one organ 'mind' (manas), which takes everything that is known as its object, which takes cognisance of past, present and future, and which assumes many functions (vṛtti).

It is this last which sometimes receives different names according to its functions, and is called manas, buddhi, ahaṅkāra or citta.[72] And in consonance with this, the Veda, after enumerating various examples of mental modes, beginning with desire, concludes 'All this is but the mind (manas)'.[73]

❖

4. And this inner organ, as an external adjunct of the soul, is called by various names at different times, such as manas, buddhi, vijñāna[74] and citta.[75] And sometimes it is given these names to indicate a particular way in which it is operating, as it is called mind (manas) when doubt (and vacillation), etc., are in play, but intellect (buddhi) when there is fixity (either of determinate cognition or will).

And the existence of an inner organ thus conceived has necessarily to be admitted. Otherwise, as the author of the Sūtras puts it, either there would always be perception or else there would be no perception at all. It would mean that whenever the soul, the sense-organs and their objects were all in relation and proximity, there would always have to be perception. Or, if on any occasion the necessary collocation of causes for perception was present and the effect did not follow, then (if there were no such extra faculty as mind) there ought never to be any perception at all. But we do not actually find this to be the case.[76]

❖

5. When food has been eaten and digested by fire in the belly, it becomes divided into three parts. The coarsest element becomes faeces. The middle element begins as liquid and becomes fat. The finest element rises upwards (from the stomach) to the heart. Following along the subtle canals called hitā, it becomes the basis of speech and other active organs, and finally becomes mind. That is to say, becoming of the nature of mind, it nourishes mind and keeps it in being. Because mind is nourished and kept in being by food, it is material, and not eternal and partless (atomic) as the

Vaiśeṣikas maintain. It is true that the text will say later that the mind is 'His divine eye',[77] but this is not because it is eternal but because it is able to reach all the objects of the senses, even the most remote. And we shall explain later how, if it is spoken of as permanent in comparison with the objects of the senses, this permanence is only relative and not absolute. For the dictum of the Veda is, 'Being is one only without a second'.[78]

❖

6. The solid component of the body is said to be composed of the element of earth, the liquid component of the element of water. Digestion, motion and the space within the hollow organs and vessels proceed from fire, wind and ether respectively.

The five senses, beginning with smell, as well as their objects, are composed of the special qualities of each of the five great elements beginning with earth respectively.[79] For the objects perceived by each sense-organ are composed of the same element as that organ, just as only light (the special quality of fire) can illumine colour (which is itself a modification of the fire-element).

These (five) sense-faculties are said to exist for the sake of knowledge, while the (five) powers of speaking, handling, walking, excretion and generation are for the sake of action. The mind (manas), standing within the whole group and constituting the eleventh faculty, selects from the reports of the other ten. The intellect (buddhi) stands for fixed determination. And finally the ultimate knower, called the Self (ātman), stands ever illumining the intellect with its own light as the latter goes on assuming different forms corresponding to the objects of its cognition. And just as light conforms to the shape of the objects it illumines and is diffused over them without mingling with them, so does the Self as knower illumine the cognitions of the intellect and conform to their shape without in fact mingling with them. Just as a stationary light illumines all that is brought near it by its mere proximity and without active effort on its part, so does the Knower clearly behold all the modifications of the intellect into the forms of sound and other objects, without activity or modification on its part.

Pleasure and pain and other (internal) qualities of the psyche characterize the intellect as identified with the totality of the individual organism and lit by the reflection of the eternal and constant light of the Self.[80] For it is on account of pains in the head and elsewhere in the body that one feels oneself to be in pain. But the knower is necessarily different from the known, the object of his knowing. From the mere fact that he takes cognisance of pain, it follows that the knower cannot himself be the one in pain. The Self becomes a sufferer through the erroneous *identification* with that which really undergoes suffering (namely the intellect), not through the mere *perception* of something in pain. Verily, the one who perceives pain in the limbs, etc. within the body is not Himself the one in pain.[81] You might say that the Self could be both the agent and the object (of the act of seeing itself in pain), like the eye (beholding itself in a mirror). But this would be wrong, for the eye is a composite entity and not a pure unity.[82]

❖

7. It follows, therefore, that there must be a special task for the Vital Energy, for the performance of which it is declared by the Veda to undergo division into five special functions called prāṇa, apāna, vyāna, udāna and samāna.[83] The prāṇa or forward-moving function is for expelling breath, etc. The apāna or downward-moving function is for inhaling breath, etc. The vyāna resides in the interval between these two (as when we hold our breath when straining) and produces vigorous action. The udāna or upward-moving function secures the withdrawal of the soul at death. The samāna or distributive function distributes sap from food to all the limbs...

And the Vital Energy in its basic form is subtle, as it also is in its specialized forms. Being subtle implies being imperceptible and limited in size, but not being (of minimal dimensions) like a primary atom. For it pervades the whole body through its five sub-divisions. It is subtle, for it is not perceived by the onlooker when it withdraws from the body at death. And we know that it must be of limited size, as there are Vedic texts speaking of it as coming and going.

It might be thought that the Vedic texts taught that it was all-pervading, as when they speak of it as 'Equal to a white ant, equal to a mosquito, equal to these three worlds, equal to all the universe'.[84] We reply that the Veda speaks of the Vital Energy as all-pervading in its divine (ādhidaivika) aspect as Hiraṇyagarbha, with its further sub-division into a single cosmic (samaṣṭi) form and a multiple individualized form (vyaṣṭi). It does not speak of the Vital Energy so when it is referring to it as it functions within the body of the individual. Moreover, in speaking of it as 'equal to a white ant, etc.', the text in question, because it uses the words 'equal to', can only be speaking of the Vital Energy in the limited form in which it exists in living beings. One cannot, therefore, raise any objection (such as saying that if it were all-pervasive it could not move, with the implication that other Vedic texts would be contradicted).[85]

❖

8. Now the text describes the Vital Energy. The forward-moving Vital Energy (prāṇa) abides in the heart and is called 'prāṇa'[86] because it tends to move forwards along the nostrils and through the mouth. The downward-moving Vital Energy (apāna) occupies the lower portion of the trunk up to the navel and is so called because it tends to draw the urine and faeces downwards. The Vital Energy producing tension (vyāna) functions in the interval between the in-going and out-going breaths and produces vigorous action. The upward-moving Vital Energy (udāna), causing elevation and rising, etc., resides in the whole of the body from the soles of the feet to the top of the head. The distributive function (samāna), so called because it promotes assimilation (sama = similar) of what has been eaten and drunk, resides in the stomach as the digestion. The Vital Energy in its most general form (ana, breath) is the general principle of which the others are particular manifestations, and is related to all the corporeal functions. All the functions as just described, from the out-going breath onwards, are nothing but the Vital Energy.[87]

❖

9. When he says 'Light, etc.,' the author of the Sūtras means that speech and the other functions are prompted to their

various activities under the control of deities identifying themselves with fire and other natural forces.

Then the author mentions the reason why this is known. He says, 'Because this is the traditional Vedic doctrine'. For there are Vedic texts on this subject, such as 'Fire (Agni), having become speech, entered the mouth'.[88] And this becoming speech and entering the mouth is predicated of the fire-deity (Agni) on the supposition that he assumes control of speech in the form of a presiding deity. For if the connection of Agni as fire-deity were denied (the Veda would stand contradicted since) no special connection of (the mere *element*) fire with speech or the mouth is perceived. And the same must be presumed to hold in the case of such texts as 'Wind (Vāyu), having become the Vital Energy, entered the nostrils'.[89] And there are other passages such as, 'Speech (Vāc) is a fourth part of the Absolute (brahman). It shines and burns with the light of fire',[90] which confirm the same idea by speaking of speech and the rest as fire and so forth. And there are yet other texts which hint at the same truth by speaking of speech and the rest as *becoming* fire and the rest, such as 'That divinity, verily, took Speech across first. When Speech was freed from death it became Fire'.[91] In all such texts we find an enumeration of speech and the various faculties on the plane of the body made to correspond with Fire and various entities on the plane of divinity, with the divinity understood to preside over the corporeal function in each case...

As for the statement made above that the senses must act unaided merely because they each have the power to fulfil their own peculiar function — it was incorrect. For we see that carts, for instance, though having the power to fulfil their own peculiar function, require to be drawn by oxen and the like.[92] And if both possibilities (i.e. that the senses were either self-propelled or else propelled by deities) are open logically, then the evidence of Vedic revelation is decisive in favour of their being impelled by deities.

It was also said that if the deities presided over the functions of the senses, the embodied soul would be deprived of its rôle as experiencer. The author of the Sūtras proceeds now to refute this notion. The revealed Vedic doctrine is that, even though the deities preside over the functioning of the sense-organs, it is the embodied soul, as being the one who possesses the Vital Energy and who is master of the entire individual organism, who effects the co-ordination of the senses one with another. For we find passages which teach that it is the embodied soul alone who effects the synthesis of the organs, such as, 'And so, whereas the organ of sight is limited to the pupil of the eye, that which has sight is the embodied soul (puruṣa), and the eye is merely his instrument for seeing. And similarly, he who has the feeling "Let me smell this" is the soul (ātman), and the sense of smell is merely his instrument'.[93] Moreover, the deities presiding over the functioning of the senses in the body could not be their experiencer on account of their plurality. For we conclude from self-recognition and other evidence that the embodied soul and experiencer in the body must be one and one only.[94]

Furthermore, it must be the embodied soul here in the body that is the constant and eternal element as the experiencer, for the embodied soul can be conceived as affected by merit and demerit and pleasure and pain, whereas the deities cannot. The latter are established on a higher plane of divine experience (aiśvarya) and cannot be supposed to stand as the experiencer in the case of the miserable body. And there is the text, 'Only the merit goes to him (Hiraṇyagarbha). No demerit goes to the gods'.[95]

❖

10. But one might ask how it could be correct to say that the various senses were quarrelling with one another and disputing who was the best, as if they were conscious human beings. How could the eye and the rest, which lack speech, engage in a verbal argument? What can it mean to say that they leave the body, then return to it again, then go to Brahmā and then sing the praises of the Vital Energy?

The answer is that speech and the rest are known to be conscious from Vedic revelation. For they are presided over by conscious deities, just like fire (agni) and the other natural forces. You might say that this conflicts with the maxim of the secular philosophers that there cannot be a plurality of conscious principles all abiding in one body (or the body would be torn apart by their conflicting wills). But this objection does not apply to our position, as we maintain that they are effectively superintended over and co-ordinated by the Lord.

Those philosophers who admit the existence of the Lord claim that all things proceed according to the rule of law because the Lord presides over them, and this holds true both of internal instruments, such as the mind, and their functions, and also of the behaviour (on the cosmic plane) of the elements, such as the earth and the rest, which build up the external world. For the regular behaviour of these is only explicable if we assume a conscious controller, as we have to do in the case of a chariot (where we assume that, because it is going in an orderly purposive way, there must be a conscious driver).

We do not, however, admit that the deities of fire and the rest are the experiencers on the individual mental plane. We take them as so many aspects of the one deity, the Cosmic Vital Energy (prāṇa), each having their own special instruments and tasks, divided a million-fold on the individual, cosmic and divine planes. And they are appointed and controlled by the Lord, for He is Himself without organs, as certain texts from the Śvetāśvatara Upanishad show, such as 'Without hands or feet, yet able to grasp and able to move swiftly', 'He sees without eyes, He hears without ears' and 'He who gave birth to Hiraṇyagarbha first of all'.[96]

❖

11. Within this body made up of food, already described, there is another self. Like the physical body, it, too, is falsely imagined to be the true Self. It is called the 'self' made up of Vital Energy (prāṇa-maya) — that is, consisting chiefly in Vital Energy. It fills the food-formed self (anna-maya, the physical body) like air filling a bellows. It assumes the form of the human body, with a head and a right side and a left side and with other features (as mentioned at Taittirīya Upanishad II.2). It does this, not spontaneously, but as conditioned by the food-formed body, which has the human form and into which it is poured like molten metal into the cast of a statue. Each self in the series (of selves to be mentioned) assumes the form of the human body through conforming to that of its

predecessor in the series. And each successive self fills its predecessor.

'The gods', proceeds the text, 'breathe in conformity with the Vital Energy'. It means that the gods like Agni breathe in conformity with the Vital Energy as it exists on the cosmic plane, the essence of the wind element, and that they actually become that principle when they breathe. They act through the activity of the Vital Energy. Or else, as the context is that of the human body, it may mean that the sense-organs, here *called* gods, perform their activities in dependence on the chief principle of Vital Energy (the mukhya-prāṇa, from which the various subordinate functions of the Vital Energy derive). All human beings and animals are able to move only through the act of breathing.

Thus it is not just as circumscribed by the self formed of food (the physical body) that living beings feel themselves to have a self. Men and animals feel themselves to have a self also on account of the 'self of Vital Energy' (prāṇa-maya-ātman), which exists within the food-formed (anna-maya) body and pervades it generally. And in the same way all living beings feel themselves to have a self also through the 'mind-self', the 'knowledge-self' and the 'bliss-self', each of which is more subtle than its predecessor in the series and pervades it, and each of which is formed from the five material elements which begin with ether, and is set up by nescience. And, over and above these, they also have a true Self which is by its very nature the cause of the ether and the other physical elements, and which is eternal and not subject to modification, all-pervading, which is defined as 'Reality, Knowledge and Infinity', and which stands beyond the five sheaths (kośa) as the Self of all. For this is the Self of all in the true sense. The last idea is included by implication....

The next 'self', the self that abides within the self of Vital Energy, is the self made up of mind (mano-maya ātman). Mind here means the organ of deliberation, etc., the inner organ. It is made up of mind as the food-formed body is made up of food....

The next in the series, that within the mind-self, is the self made up of knowledge (vijñāna-maya ātman). The knowledge-self is that which exists within the mind-self. The mind-self is said to be that which can assume the form of the Vedic texts (without yet fully comprehending them). But 'knowledge' (vijñāna) here means final knowledge of matters contained in the Veda. This knowledge, known as definite determination (adhyavasāya), is a property of the inner organ (antaḥ-karaṇa). The self made up of this knowledge, formed, that is, of definite cognitions arrived at through critical application of the means of knowledge (pramāṇa), is called the 'self of knowledge'. Ritualistic sacrifices and the like can only be performed through definite knowledge based on the critical application of the means of knowledge, as the text will later explain....[97]

The phrase (in regard to the next 'self') 'made up of bliss' shows that we are (still) dealing (not with the transcendent 'causal' Self but) with a 'self belonging to the realm of effects'. This is already clear from the context[98] and from the presence of the words 'made up of'. The self made up of food and the rest are the subject-matter now being treated of, and these are 'selves' belonging to the realm of effects and formed from the material elements. The self made up of bliss falls within this series. And the suffix 'maya' (in 'ānanda-maya') is here used in the sense of 'a modification of', just as it is in the case of the word 'anna-maya' (made up of food). Hence the self made up of bliss must be taken as a self belonging to the realm of effects....

Bliss is the fruit of meditation and rituals. 'Made up of bliss' means a modification of that bliss. And this 'self of bliss' lies within the 'self of knowledge'. For the present text implies that the self of bliss lies within the self of knowledge and is the cause of the performance of ritualistic sacrifices, etc. For the fruit of meditation on the symbolic significance of rituals and of the performance of ritual must be taken as 'innermost', for it is that which exists directly for the sake of the experiencer. And the bliss self is more internal than the other selves which preceded it in the series.

Moreover, meditation and rituals are performed for the sake of joy in its various grades to be detailed below, and that is the only reason why they are performed at all. Because joy and its various grades, the fruits of meditation and rituals, are intimately connected with the Self, it is but right to regard them as more internal than the self of knowledge. In dream one experiences the bliss-self, arising from the latent impressions of the various grades of joy that (come then to) penetrate the knowledge-self.[99]

Joy, such as the joy of seeing a beloved son, etc., is the head of the self made up of bliss. That is to say, it is *like* the head, because it is the chief element in it. The word 'moda' means the state of joy following on the acquisition of something dear. The word 'pramoda' means delight, or the extreme form of this emotion. The word 'ānanda' (bliss) means the 'self' or common form of the various grades of joy, being interwoven with all of them.

Bliss really means the Absolute in its supreme form. For that is what manifests in that clear state of the inner organ, unclouded by darkness, that arises when, under the influence of its past good deeds, some dear object like a son or a friend comes before it. And this is what is known in the world as pleasure derived from objects. But because the good deeds that brought about that state of the inner organ were but casual, the joy to be derived from them is fleeting. The more the inner organ is purified through ascetic practices designed to destroy ignorance, through symbolic meditation ordained in the Veda (vidyā), through continence and fervour, the greater degree of bliss it will contain. For the text will say later on, 'He is the sap. Having acquired the sap, one feels joy. He it is who causes joy'. Or, as another text puts it, 'Other creatures live on a fraction of this bliss'. And, in harmony with this, the present text will say later that bliss becomes greater and greater a hundred-fold each time that one rises above certain types of desire.

But the Absolute is superior to the bliss-self, which, if one compares (and contrasts) it with the (bliss experienced in the) concrete realization of the Absolute, the final reality, is something that is seen to increase by stages. That which was introduced by the definition 'Reality, Knowledge, Infinity', that for the sake of the realization of which the whole doctrine of the five sheaths was instituted (not as a statement of the truth but as a practical device for elevating the pupil on the path), that which stands within the sheaths (in so far as they exist at all), that in virtue of which they 'exist' and 'have a self' — that is the Absolute, the 'tail', the support. The Absolute is the non-dual support of all, in the sense of being the limiting-point beyond which negation of the appearance of duality set up by nescience can never go.[100]

❖

12. The seventeen-fold[101] subtle body (liṅga-śarīra) lies in these subtle passages (nāḍī) which are of the diameter of the thousandth part of a hair-tip and pervade the body, carrying their white, blue, brown, green and red matter.[102] In the subtle body lie all the latent impressions (vāsanā) springing from the good and evil experiences of transmigratory life. This subtle body, the abode of the impressions, which is (by nature) transparent as crystal on account of its subtlety, experiences contact in dreams with the external adjunct consisting of the traces of its former experiences that are lodged in the subtle canals (nāḍī). It then assumes various modifications arising under the influence of merit and demerit from past deeds, and adopts forms from its past experience, such as women, chariots, elephants and the like.[103]

❖

13. And this fire, along with the other subtle elements that form the vehicle for the soul when it vacates the present body, must be of subtle (imperceptible) consistency, both from the point of view of its intangible nature and dimensions. For there are texts saying that it emerges from the body through the subtle physical canals (nāḍī), which show that it must be subtle, since it could only pass along these if it were subtle in form. It is on account of its intangibility that it knows no

physical obstructions. Hence, also, the fact that the bystanders cannot perceive it when it issues forth from the body (at death). Hence, too, the fact that it is not destroyed when the gross body is destroyed by burning on the funeral pyre or otherwise.

Further, the warmth that people feel when they touch this gross body is the warmth of this subtle body alone. For at death, even though the gross body remains in being along with its properties, such as colour and form, heat is not perceived there, but only in the gross body in its living condition. Hence it follows that this heat must reside in something other than the familiar gross body (i.e. in the subtle body, which must consequently exist). And the Veda confirms this idea in the text, 'It is warm as long as it lives and cold when it dies'.[104]

❖

14. He, the Self, 'went round on all sides', that is, He pervaded all like the ether. 'White' or 'pure' means luminous, that is 'flashing'. 'Bodiless' means without a body, that is, without a subtle body (liṅga-śarīra). 'Having no apertures and no passages'. These last two characteristics show that He has no gross physical body. 'Pure' means unsoiled by nescience. He has no causal body (kāraṇa-śarīra).[105]

❖

15. If the soul were an agent by nature it could never be liberated from agency, any more than fire can be liberated from being hot. Nor can one who is not liberated from agency be shown to have attained the highest human goal, for agency is painful by nature.

The case, indeed, can be illustrated by the everyday example of a carpenter, who becomes an agent and suffers pain when he takes his chisel and other instruments in hand, and yet when he has returned home and put down his chisel becomes himself again, relaxed, at rest and happy. In the same way the soul, in the states of waking and dream, becomes interpenetrated by duality set up by nescience, and becomes an agent and suffers pain. And then afterwards, to shake off its weariness, it enters into its own Self,[106] the Absolute, the transcendent, takes leave of the psycho-physical organism, and becomes a non-agent and feels happy in the state of highest serenity (dreamless sleep).[107] And in the same way, in the state of liberation, too, having removed the darkness of nescience with the lamp of spiritual knowledge, the Self remains in the state of transcendence, contented and happy.

The relevance of the example of the state of the carpenter is limited to the following. It is only in his special activities such as the actual act of carpentry that the carpenter is here regarded as an agent, and then only with the aid of tools such as the chisel. Limited to his body alone, he is not an agent (*qua* carpenter). In the same way, the Self is an agent in all its worldly activities only through resorting to its instruments in the psycho-physical organism, such as the mind. In itself it is not an agent. But the analogy should not be pressed too far, as it is not intended to say that the Self has limbs like the carpenter, such as the hands with which he grasps his tools, wherewith to lay down or take up its instruments such as the mind.

As for the statement that agency must belong to the soul by nature on such grounds as the argument that the Veda could not be meaningful in any other way — that was wrong. The part of the Veda that deals with injunctions and prohibitions accepts agency as empirically presented and then teaches particular duties. It does not proclaim that the soul actually *is* an agent. And we have already explained how the soul cannot be an agent by nature from the very fact that the Veda teaches that it is the Absolute. Thus the part of the Veda that deals with injunctions and prohibitions proceeds on the basis of accepting agency as we find it, though it is only set up by nescience.... And this also refutes the thesis that the individual soul must be an agent by nature as it is referred to as 'wandering (at will in dream)' and as 'taking (the sense-organs with him in dream as a great king takes his retinue)'.[108] For these texts, too, are not statements of fact, but adaptations of the truth in conformity with the hearer's experience.[109]

❖

16. 'Being open' and 'being closed' are states (of the physical eye) animated by the Vital Energy, and they occur at a particular place (*viz.* within the eye-socket). They are not states of the faculty of vision itself, which is of the nature of (permanent and unchanging) light. Nor do they affect the lower mind or the higher mind, as these, too, are of the nature of light.[110] What belong to the lower mind and higher mind are thought and knowledge respectively. The properties of all these faculties are mutually distinct, yet all are superimposed indiscriminately onto the Self. The range of perception of the senses is limited by their position (in a particular body). The intellect identifies itself with them. The Knower, beholding the intellect (as itself an object) seems to be limited to the body.[111]

3. The Light that Illumines the Soul

The Extracts of the present section develop the same theme that we have already met with in Volume I, Chapter IV, section 3 above. But whereas the Extracts in that series were more metaphysical in flavour, those of the present section are more descriptive and psychological in character. They do not merely state that our experiences force us to conclude that an unchanging, self-luminous principle must exist within the individual as the Witness of his passing states of experience. They go on further to suggest that it is the presence of this light which unifies and organizes the psychic and physical functions and enables perception and other cognitive acts to take place.

The first Extract argues from the principle, already familiar from Chapter VIII, section 2, above, that the mind and senses are composed of the material elements, and that there must exist some self-luminous light perceiving them if there is to be experience at all. The second Extract depicts the intellect as the chief instrument of this self-luminous principle in the case of the waking experience of an ordinary unenlightened man. The third Extract differentiates the Self from the mind and its ego-notion.

Extracts 4 to 6 enter, as far as it interested Śaṅkara to go, into the epistemology of perception. It is clear that the account of the mechanism of sight found in Śaṅkara's texts, in which the mind, lit by a reflection of consciousness, reaches out across space through the sense-organ to enwrap the distant object, will not do, as it stands, for the modern age. But whatever modifications and elaboration may be required in the account of the mechanism of the senses, the view that consciousness, itself static, illumines the mind, and, being reflected in the mind, illumines the sense-organ and ultimately the object, cannot be ruled out *a priori* as an untenable hypothesis.

Extract 4 argues that the fact that we dream and remember is only explicable if it is taken that the mind assumes the form of what it perceives in the waking state. Extract 5 explains perception in the waking state as implying that the mind does indeed conform to the shape of the object and that what is perceived *directly* is the mental image. Extract 6 elaborates and sums up all that has gone before, being a key passage for Śaṅkara's epistemology and for the metaphysical implications he drew from it.[112] According to this passage, the intellect is the special and most intimate instrument of the Self in empirical knowledge. The intellect is lit by the light of the Self, and objects are lit by the intellect through the medium of the senses, and require to be so lit in order to be perceived at all. The light of the Self within is reflected in the intellect, and this reflected light is passed on, by contact (samparka), to the lower mind, senses and the body. People identify themselves with this or that aspect of the psycho-physical organism, depending on how far their powers of discrimination have developed and rescued them from crude self-identification with the body. As long as there is failure to discriminate the Self from the intellect, the Self appears 'like' the appearances that come before it. But in truth it is pure light and does not really act or move.

TEXTS ON THE LIGHT THAT ILLUMINES THE SOUL

1. How is that to be known, knowing which the enlightened ones (Brāhmaṇa) desire nothing more? The reply begins by referring to that Self, of the nature of Consciousness, through which everyone in the world has their clear knowledge of colour, taste, odour, sound, touch and the joys of sex-contact.

Perhaps you will object that people do not have the feeling 'I experience knowledge through the Self which transcends the body and the mind'. What everyone feels is, 'It is I, the one consisting of body, mind and senses, who am the one who has knowledge'. But this objection is not right. For the body, mind and senses, being themselves nothing other than modifications of the cosmic elements,[113] and being themselves knowable objects, cannot be the knower. If, indeed, the body-mind complex, being itself composed of (fire with its quality of) colour and the other elements (with their respective qualities), were capable (on its own) of knowing colour and the (qualities of the) other elements, then the external objects of the world would also know both each other and themselves. But we do not find this to be the case.

The truth is, therefore, that everyone in the world enjoys knowledge of (fire with the quality of) colour, and also the other elements composing the body, through another principle that is different from them and is pure Consciousness by very nature. It is comparable to the case where we say, 'That *by virtue of which* the iron burns anything is fire'.[114]

What exceptions are there, asks the text, to the law that all is known by the Self? There are no exceptions. All is known by the Self. The Self which knows all things without exception is omniscient.[115]

❖

2. We are aware of two entities within the body, an instrument which assumes various different forms and *through which* we have empirical knowledge, and a single (changeless) principle which has knowledge. We are assured of the presence of the latter, since we are able to remember objects perceived by various different organs. That *through which* knowledge takes place cannot be the Self.[116]

But what, exactly, is the instrument through which we acquire empirical knowledge? It is said here to be that (instrument of cognition) which becomes the eye (sense of sight) to enable us to apprehend colour, and which becomes the ear (sense of hearing) to enable us to apprehend sound, and which becomes the sense of smell to enable us to apprehend odours, and which becomes the faculty of speech to enable us to express concepts (nāma) such as 'cow' or 'horse' or to express our feelings in ejaculations like 'Bravo! Bravo!'[117] and which becomes the sense of taste to enable us to savour tastes, sweet and bitter.

But what exactly, is that one instrument of cognition that assumes these various forms? The reply given is that it was said before[118] that the essence of man was the heart, the essence of the heart was mind, that Varuṇa and the waters were created by mind, that mind arose from the heart, and the moon from mind. Thus heart and mind are but one substance in two forms. Through this one inner organ (antaḥ-karaṇa), when it becomes the eye (sense of sight), one sees colours; when it becomes the ear, one hears; when it becomes the sense of smell, one smells; when it becomes the organ of speech, one talks; when it becomes the sense of taste, one enjoys savour; when it retains its natural form as mind, one vacillates; and when it becomes the heart (intellect, buddhi), one makes fixed determinations and firm decisions. Hence it is this one instrument operating in the sphere of all the different organs that serves the knower in his knowledge of all objects.

And in a similar way we find in the Kauṣītaki Upanishad such texts as 'Entering speech as consciousness (prajñā), He attains to all names through speech... Entering the eye (sense of sight) as consciousness, He attains all forms'.[119] And in the Bṛhadāraṇyaka Upanishad we find, 'Through the mind alone does He see, through the mind does He hear' and 'He knows forms through the heart (intellect)'.[120] Hence we accept that it is the organ known variously as mind or intellect that is the instrument in all empirical knowledge. And the Vital Energy is identical with it. For there is the Vedic text, 'That which is called Vital Energy (prāṇa) is consciousness (prajñā) and that which is called consciousness is the Vital Energy....'[121]

The Self has to be taken as that knower for whose sake the intellect assumes, as instrument, the various functions we are about to describe. The Knower, the Absolute, pure Consciousness, rests in that external adjunct called the inner organ (antaḥ-karaṇa). In order to minister to its empirical experience, the inner organ is said to assume the following modes to convey both external objects and mental states: alertness, authority to command, artistic talent, brilliance, retentiveness, perceptiveness, buoyancy to spur on the senses and body when they flag as when we say 'They are buoying up their spirits', thoughtfulness, the spirit of independence, gloom arising from illness or the like, memory, the power to summon up vivid pictures, resolution, liveliness, desire for what one has not got (kāma)[122] and passion in the form of hankering for women and the like. These and others are the modes of the inner organ. They exist for the sake of the experience of the knower, who is the Absolute (brahman) as pure Consciousness, and are his external adjuncts. Hence it comes about that, as consciousness, He receives by transference the names that apply to the qualities arising from His adjuncts,[123] but they do not describe Him directly as He is.[124]

3. He is the best of the knowers of the Absolute who knows himself to be the one Self, everywhere the same, as the Lord Vāsudeva declared himself to be one and the same in his own body (into which He 'descended' as Kṛṣṇa) and in a fig-tree. Just as you do not admit that you have the feeling 'I' or 'mine' in relation to the bodies of others, so, in the same way, even in this body you are only the Witness of the intellect. There is no difference between the two cases. Attachment, aversion, fear and other qualities of the intellect are perceived as located in the intellect along with the representations of external objects and memory impressions. Hence the Knower, (who witnesses them as objects and therefore is distinct from them Himself), is ever pure and free from fear.

The doctrine that he who meditates on a deity becomes that deity applies only in the realm of difference: no action is required on one's own Self to make it become the Self. Since one is already one's own Self without dependence on external means, one's own Self cannot be something which requires means for its realization. The Self as pure Consciousness is homogeneous like the ether. As associated with external adjuncts such as the eye, its nature is wrongly conceived. The ego-notion we have is not a characteristic of the Self, since it is perceived as an object like a pot. This applies equally to all other notions and imperfections of the mind. For the Self is taintless.

Moreover, being the Witness (sākṣin) of *all* other cognitions, it is itself changeless and omnipresent. If the Witness underwent modification of any kind, its range of knowledge would be limited, like that of the mind and sense-organs. But there is no break in the seeing of the Seer, as there is in that of the eye and the other organs....

One should reflect over the problem of one's own nature. Am I the totality of all matter and of all organs of cognition everywhere taken collectively? Or am I this same totality taken (pluralistically) as separate in all distinct parts? Or am I but one part of it, and, if so, which part? I am neither matter nor the organs of cognition, whether taken collectively or individually. For matter forms the object of my knowledge, and the organs are the instruments through which I know. The Knower must be different from the instruments and objects of his knowledge, as (the conscious seer of a pot is different from) a pot.

The Self is the fire. The intellect is the fuel. Fanned by nescience, desire and action, the flames shoot out through the windows of the senses. Even the intellect is active in the senses, of which the right eye is the chief; it flares up with the oblations of the sense-objects. Then the fire of the Self enjoys the gross objects of waking experience. When, at the time of perceiving colour and other sense-objects, the Self remains void of attachment, thinking 'Oblations are being offered into a fire', then it is not soiled by the evils of the waking condition. When, in the dream-state, the Self stands revealed to view in the picture-gallery of the mind, beholding the images arising from the latent impressions (vāsanā) generated by nescience and past action, it is called 'the bright-one' (taijasa). It is self-luminous and itself illumines the objects of its vision. When (in dreamless sleep) neither objects nor impressions are being stirred forth from the mind through the influence of past actions, then the Self is known as 'the All-luminous One (prājña)'. For it sees nothing but its own

Self.[125] The mind, the senses and the intellect assume their various states through the influence of past actions, and are illumined by pure Consciousness, as pots and other objects are illumined by the sun.

This being so, the Self, as Knower, merely illumines the various cognitions by his light. Fools say that He is the agent in these acts of cognition, which exist purely for his sake. True, He is called 'omniscient'. But this only means that all is illumined by His light.[126] And because He is that on which all action depends, He is spoken of (figuratively) as 'the universal agent'. But the Self is only spoken of thus by virtue of his adjuncts. In His own true nature, apart from external adjuncts, He is indescribable. Pure, partless and without qualities — mind and speech cannot reach Him. He is called variously conscious, non-conscious, an agent, a non-agent, pervasive, non-pervasive, bound, free, one, many, pure, impure. 'Words fall back from the Self, together with the mind, without having reached it',[127] since it is without qualities, without action and without any particular characteristics.[128]

One should know the Self, in isolation from its illusory adjuncts, as the ultimate Ground. Like the ether, it is all-pervading yet unrelated to solid objects. Endowed with the all-seeing light, one should reject all that is perceived (in the waking state), all that is remembered (as in dream) and also the darkness (of dreamless sleep), as the sun dispels the darkness of night. That which is the ultimate Witness of the cognitions bearing upon the forms (of the waking world), upon memory (as in dream) and upon darkness (in dreamless sleep) is the sole true Self, Omnipresent, the Perceiver, the same in all beings.[129]

4. In dream and memory we see the mere appearance of the form of an object such as a pot (and not any external pot existing and present at the time). And we infer that a mental presentation having the form of a pot must have been previously seen (even in the earlier waking experience).

Just as (when an ascetic dreams of himself as begging) the body seen in dream as wandering forth begging is not the dreamer himself, so is the latter different from his body as perceived in the waking state, too. For (it is perceived and) he is the perceiver.

Molten bronze poured into a mould assumes the form of the latter. Similarly, the mind, penetrating to the objects of perception such as colour, etc., is seen to assume their form. Or again, just as light, as revealer, assumes the form of that which it reveals, so the mind is seen in the form of all objects, since it reveals all objects. What the Spirit in man formerly perceived as the object was in fact the intellect itself, which had assumed the form of the object. Otherwise, how could he again perceive it in dream? Or how could there be memory? The intellect 'reveals' objects only in the sense that it is seen as an object whose form it has assumed, while the Self is a 'perceiver' by virtue of pervading the intellect on the rise of a particular modification of the latter.

Because all cognitions of all living beings are illumined by me as the light of pure Consciousness, I am the Self of all. In dream, the agent, the act, the instrument, the object and the fruit of action are all modifications of the intellect, and the same is also true of the waking state. The permanent Witness of both states must therefore be different in nature from the intellect and its modifications.[130]

5. What kind of a relation can there be between the ultimate Knower, who is the Seer, and the thing known, the seen (the mental cognition), other than that of Seer and seen (subject and object)? Is the act of seeing performed by the Knower? Or does it actively pervade the object? No. The truth is that a certain support, merely, is given to the mental cognitions by the constant and changeless Knower (through his mere inactive presence).

We have already said that this 'support' consists in the acquisition by the intellect of a reflection of Consciousness. Thus equipped with a reflection of Consciousness, the intellect encompasses pots and other objects as their illuminator, just as light, for example, encompasses the objects that it illumines. A pot becomes invested with the intellect in perception in just the same way as it is invested with light when it is standing in light. The investing of the pot with the intellect is the 'encompassing by the intellect' (dhī-vyāpti).

'Encompassing by the intellect' is a process which has stages. First there is the encompassing of the pot by the mental modification, and afterwards comes the 'support' of the Self (in the form of a reflection or semblance of consciousness). But one cannot attribute participation in any process to the one Witness of all, any more than to time and space (or other receptacles of change).[131]

❖

6. The Self is referred to by the word 'this' because it is immediately evident. It is here called 'composed of knowledge' because, having entered into apparent conjunction with its external adjunct, the intellect, it is not discriminated from

it. For the Self can only be an apprehender when it is in conjunction with the intellect, as the demon Rāhu[132] can only be seen when it is in conjunction with the moon and the sun (in an eclipse). The intellect serves the Self for all its purposes, like a lamp set in front of one in the dark, as the Upanishad has already said in the words, 'It is through the mind alone that one sees, through the mind that one hears'.[133]

Objects are only perceived when invested with the light of the intellect. It is as if they were standing in the dark and were perceived only as lit by the light of some lamp held in front of them. The other sense-organs are to be regarded as mere channels serving the intellect. That is why the Veda speaks of the Self as qualified by the intellect alone and calls it 'Vijñāna-maya'....

The word 'amidst' in the phrase 'amidst the sense-organs' shows that the Self is different from them. It implies proximity, as in the phrase 'a tree amidst the rocks'. People are by no means sure whether the Self is or is not different from the organs, and by saying 'amidst the sense-organs' the text means to point out that it *is* different. That which is *amidst* other things is itself different from them, like a tree *amidst* the rocks....

Or we might illustrate the matter in another way. An emerald or other precious stone, when thrown into milk or the like to test it, imparts its own peculiar sheen to the milk. In a similar way, the light of the Self, being more subtle even than the intellect, the heart, stands within the heart and unifies the heart and the whole assemblage of organs and limbs, imparting to them the sheen of its own light. For it is the inmost principle of all, and they transmit this sheen one to another, since they form a hierarchical series descending from the more subtle to the more gross.

The intellect receives a reflection of the light of the Self as pure Consciousness first, since it is transparent and stands in immediate proximity to the Self. Hence even persons of discrimination identify themselves initially[134] with the intellect. Consciousness next illumines the lower mind,[135] as the next inmost principle, mediately through its contact with the intellect. Next it illumines the sense-organs mediately through its contact with the mind, and next the body through its contact with the sense-organs. And in this way the entire psycho-physical organism is illumined by the light of pure Consciousness in successive stages. And thus it is that everyone identifies himself with this or that part of the psycho-physical organism, and with this or that function of its various organs, according to the progress in or limitations of his powers of discrimination....

The Spirit (within the heart) is called 'Puruṣa' because it is infinite (pūrṇa),[136] being all-pervading like the ether. And its self-luminosity is perfect (pūrṇa), because it illumines all else without itself being illumined by any other principle. And it is the Spirit, of the very nature of self-existent light, which is the answer to the question (put by King Janaka to Yājña-valkya), 'Which Self (is the ultimate light in man)?' The point being made is that when all the external lights that aid the senses have subsided, the light within the heart, the Spirit, the Self, illumines the senses through the medium of the inner organ. Even when the sun and other external aids to the senses are present, the psycho-physical organism cannot enjoy experience without the help of the Self, whose light does not exist for the sake of another. For the psycho-physical organism *per se* is without consciousness, and the light of the sun and other external luminaries exists for the sake of another.[137] All experience everywhere depends on the light of the Self.... All the experience of living beings is based on illusory self-identification. And we have explained the manner of this through the example of the emerald....

It is the intellect (or heart) to which the Self has been said to be similar. What does this 'similarity' imply? It means that they are not separately distinguishable, like horse and buffalo. The intellect is illumined, and the light of the Self is what illumines it like (ordinary) light illumining an object. It is well-known that one cannot distinguish (light as) the illuminator from what it illumines, for its very clarity renders light similar to whatever it illumines. Whatever colour light illumines, it becomes like that colour and assumes its hue, becoming green, blue or red whenever it illumines those colours. And it is in the same way that the Self illumines the intellect and thought, and through them, the whole of the psycho-physical organism, as we have explained by the example of the emerald. The Self becomes 'like all this' through its similarity to the intellect. So the text will say of it later, 'identified with all'.[138]

Thus it is not possible to separate the Self from anything and exhibit it in its true nature as pure light, as one can separate the stalk of the muñja grass from its outer covering (and hold it up to view). And hence it is that everyone superimposes every kind of activity, which really belongs to the realm of name and form, onto the Self, and superimposes the property of light (which really belongs to the Self alone) onto name and form. And since people thus superimpose name and form onto the Self-of-the-nature-of-Light, they become utterly confused by alternative fancies such as 'This is my Self', 'No, it is not the Self', 'The Self is of such and such a nature', 'No, it is not of that nature', 'It is an agent', 'It is not an agent', 'It is pure', 'It is not pure', 'It is bound', 'It is free', 'It is motionless', 'It moves', 'It exists', 'It does not exist'.

Hence, because it assumes the appearance of the intellect, the Self appears to move to and fro between the two worlds. That is to say, it moves to and fro between this world, which it has already attained, and the next world which has to be attained in the future, by giving up the aggregate of the body, the senses and the rest which it has already acquired, and assuming others through a stream of hundreds of continuous changes. And this moving to and fro between the two worlds takes place (as an illusion) caused by the similarity of the Self to the intellect. It does not really take place at all....

And the text proceeds to show that this is a matter of experience by saying 'Hence it "appears" to meditate', to perform the activity of meditating or pondering. The meaning is that it illumines the intellect, which does have the power of performing meditation, with its light, which is of the nature of pure Consciousness. And then being *like* (i.e. indistinguishable from) the intellect, it appears to meditate, just as light (appears to move when the things it illumines move). So the notion that the Self really ponders is just a popular error. And it is the same with the text, 'He appears to move', where 'move' means to undergo vigorous movements. When the intellect and the other organs and the Vital Energies undergo motion, then the Self *appears* to move, as it is *like* them (indistinguishable from them) and it is therefore identified with them because it illumines them. But that Light of the Self does not really have the property of movement.[139]

4. The Soul and the Lord are not Distinct

There are texts in the Upanishads and in the Epics and Purāṇas, including the Gītā, which imply that the individual soul is different from the Lord and that he should approach Him in devotion and that he may perhaps attain to Him or to 'his world' through his grace. For Śaṅkara, these texts had validity within the world of nescience. But if they were to be taken as the final truth, they would conflict with the other texts speaking of the utter transcendence of the one and only non-dual Self, bereft of all duality and all empirically knowable characters. Śaṅkara devoted considerable effort to showing how the former texts were only provisional in character, designed to suit the beliefs of the student before he was ready to pass on to the higher stages of the discipline. It seems likely that many of the objections he answers — for instance the charge that his doctrine of the identity of the individual soul and the Lord renders the Veda valueless — were objections actually raised against him by the opponents of Advaita in his own day.

It is proposed in the present section to give a few examples from Śaṅkara's texts describing the relation between the individual soul and the Lord. Extracts 1 to 4 show that while the individual soul *in its true nature* is identical with (is nothing other than) the Lord, the Lord in his true nature is not identical with the individual soul in its individual nature. In particular, the Lord is not in his true nature the transmigrant, though He may appear to be the transmigrant on account of external adjuncts which do not affect his real nature. Extract 5 shows that the individual soul is dependent on the Lord for his power to act. Extracts 6 to 9 show how the relation between the individual soul and the Lord appears different from different standpoints. From the standpoint of nescience they may seem different, and identity with the Lord then appears to be a 'goal' that has to be 'attained'. From the standpoint of knowledge, this identity is a fact. Bondage and liberation, in turn, depend on whether the student feels himself to be different from or identical with the Lord.

TEXTS ON THE SOUL AND THE LORD AS NOT DISTINCT

1. The Teacher Kāśakṛtsna holds that this[140] is but an expedient to teach non-difference, since the supreme Self also exists as the Self-of-the-nature-of-Consciousness (vijñāna-ātman).[141] And there are texts like 'Let Me enter as the living soul and bring out name and form into manifestation'[142] which show that the supreme Self exists also as the individual soul.... When (in the above-quoted passage from the Chāndogya Upanishad) the Veda speaks of the creation of fire and the other elements, it does not mention any separate creation of the individual soul as if it were anything other than the supreme Self, or as if it were, for instance, a modification (vikāra) of some kind arising from it. The view of the Teacher Kāśakṛtsna is that the individual soul *is* the supreme Lord Himself.

As for Āśmarathya, he holds, it is true, that the individual soul is non-different from the supreme Self. But he only does so from one particular point of view, the point of view, namely, 'that the promise might be kept'.[143] He therefore continues to hold, also, that the supreme Self and the individual soul are in some sense cause and effect (and therefore to some extent necessarily different). In Auḍulomi's doctrine, the individual soul is quite clearly spoken of as being *both* different from *and* identical with the supreme Self, these being the two *conditions* of the individual soul (according to whether it has or has not attained release).

Of these three views, it is that of Kāśakṛtsna which really follows the Veda, since it follows the final truth which the Veda aims to convey, as in such texts as 'That thou art'.[144] And that is why the individual soul could be spoken of as immortal.[145] This would not be so, for instance, if the individual soul were taken as a modification of the Self, for any modification is bound to be dissolved sooner or later into its material cause. And for the same reason it follows that name and form, since they cannot rest in the individual soul in its true nature, rest in its accidental adjunct (upādhi), and are only to be attributed to the individual soul figuratively. And again, when the Veda appeals to such examples as sparks arising from fire and says, on this analogy, that the individual soul is produced (from the Self as a modification of the latter) these statements also, have to be understood as applying to the external adjuncts only....

Objection: But we have declarations that the individual undergoes destruction, in such texts as 'Having arisen from out of these elements, he is eventually destroyed and dissolved back into them. There is no consciousness after death'.[146] How, then, can you say that the individual soul is non-different from the supreme Self?

Answer: There is nothing wrong here. When there is mention in this text of 'destruction' it means that there is destruction of all particularized consciousness, not that the (soul as the) Self undergoes destruction.... For the reply is given, 'Come, I am not saying anything to bewilder you. Verily, this Self is indestructible, and its nature (as Consciousness) is indestructible too. But it becomes disconnected from the organs'.[147]

What it means is this. This Self, as a mass of Consciousness, is verily eternal and constant. It cannot be destroyed. But its connection with the organs, which are composed of the elements and set up by nescience, is dissolved through knowledge. When the text says, 'There is no consciousness after death', what it means is that when the Self is disconnected from the organs it has no particularized consciousness, since the latter arises from that source....

We have the text, 'Where there is the appearance of duality, there a person sees an object as something different from himself'[148] which refers to the realm of nescience and to the particularized consciousness manifesting in sight and other sense-faculties, which belong to that realm alone. But then, in the words 'But when for him everything has become the Self alone, then what could he see and with what?', the passage goes on to declare how in the realm of enlightenment the particularized consciousness associated with sight and other sense-faculties does not exist. And then again, in answer to the doubt whether, even in the absence of objects, he might not take active cognisance of the Self, the text goes on to say, 'Through what could he know the Knower?' This last passage is there to give the reason for the absence of particularized consciousness. So it follows that the reference is to pure Being only, as the root of the act of knowing, and that it is referred to with a verbal suffix as 'knower' only in respect of its former (unenlightened) state as the individual soul.

And we have already shown how it is Kāśakṛtsna's doctrine that really conforms to the Veda. The distinction, therefore, between the supreme Self and the individual soul is not ultimately true. It is caused by the presence of the accidental defining adjuncts, such as the body, senses and mind, which consist in name and form, which are themselves set up by nescience. And this is the doctrine which is proclaimed by all the upanishadic texts (when properly interpreted as constituting a single ordered whole).[149]

❖

2. It is true that there is no being subject to transmigration who is (in the true metaphysical sense) distinct from the Lord. But our doctrine makes provision for a 'relation' (of the Self) with the external adjunct consisting of the psycho-physical organism, just as the ether 'comes into relation' with different kinds of pots and mountain caves and other (hollow) adjuncts. And we find that this gives rise to various empirical notions, such as 'the volume of ether enclosed by the clay pot' or 'the volume of ether enclosed by the coconut-shell water-vessel', where neither of these are anything other than the universal ether. And this gives rise to the false notion of a separate volume of ether pertaining to each of the clay pots and other vessels. And in the same way in the case of the Absolute, too, there is the false notion of a distinction between souls on the one hand and 'the Lord' on the other, arising from a failure to distinguish the Self from its form as related to the external

adjunct of the body and the organs. Although all that truly exists is the Self, there is the persistent tendency to attribute selfhood to the complex of the body and organs through a series of mere (interdependent) false cognitions. It is only in the case of one who becomes a transmigrant in this sense that 'taking thought'[150] would depend on a body and organs.[151]

❖

3. But may we not suppose that the individual soul passes into a different state and ceases to be a transmigrant (and becomes the Lord)? That self-consisting-of-consciousness, which in the waking state experiences the objects of the world composed of the elements, assumes a different state called 'dreamless sleep' in which it is no longer the transmigrant but the Supreme, the Controller, quite other than the individual soul.

No. We cannot allow this view to stand.[152] For it implies something which is contrary to all experience. For no object is found to have qualities which behave like that (i.e. which change and disappear) outside the theories of the Buddhist Nihilists. We do not find in ordinary worldly dealings that a cow is a cow when it is standing or walking, but suddenly becomes a horse or some completely different species when it lies down. And the opponent's view is also contradicted by all sound logic. For whatever object is critically determined to have a given characteristic as an essential property retains that characteristic through all changes of time and place. If it could lose it, all critical knowledge would be at an end.[153]

It is true that the Sāṅkhyas and Mīmāṃsakas and other

(atheistic) philosophers, trained in logic, produce hundreds of arguments to show that there is no transcendent (i.e. non-transmigrant) Self at all. But this view (which implies that the whole world proceeds from the actions of the individual selves undergoing transmigration) is wrong. For the soul undergoing transmigration does not possess the knowledge to be the agent in producing the rise, maintenance and dissolution of the universe. Nor was there any truth in the view you elaborated so minutely that it is the transmigrant himself, the experiencer of the objects of the external world composed of the elements, who attains to another state and creates the world. For everyone can see immediately that no one undergoing transmigration possesses the means, power or knowledge to effect the creation, maintenance and withdrawal of the world. No person undergoing transmigration like us could even conceive of the disposition of the different material elements mentally, let alone create the universe....

Objection: The Absolute, which is not the one undergoing transmigration, is the cause of the universe. It is eternally pure, enlightened and liberated by nature and beyond hunger and thirst, while the one undergoing transmigration is the reverse of all this, and ought not to think 'I am the Absolute'. How could the humble transmigrant fail to incur sin by thinking of himself as the Supreme, as a god and as the Lord?

Therefore (the objector continues) the right course for the one undergoing transmigration is to offer worship to the Lord with flowers, water offered in cupped hands, hymns, inclinations of the body, sacrificial offerings, charity, recitations, meditation, yoga and other practices. One who knows the Absolute through worship *becomes* the Absolute, the Ruler of All. But one should not meditate on the Absolute, which is transcendent, as identical with the one under transmigration. For this would be like meditating on fire as cold or on ether as palpable. Those parts of the Veda which teach that the Absolute is the Self of man should be disregarded as mere eulogies. And in this way one will avoid conflict with trained philosophers of all schools and with the common-sense of mankind.

Answer: This is wrong. For we have Vedic passages in both prose and verse which declare that the Supreme entered the human body (to form the individual soul, which is consequently identical with Him).... And it is to be noted that the term 'Self' (ātman) is found used throughout the Veda for the Absolute (brahman), and the word 'Self' means the inmost Self, so that there is no being separate from the supreme Self undergoing transmigration.[154]

❖

4. *Objection:* Your statement that the individual souls undergoing transmigration are not different, at bottom, from the Lord, was wrong. The fact is that the Lord and the individual soul are distinct, as they have distinct characteristics, like a horse and a buffalo. The Lord has constant knowledge of all objects, comparable to the light of the sun, whereas the knowledge of the soul undergoing transmigration is the very opposite of that, like the light of a firefly. The range of their power is different, too. The power of the Lord is eternal and embraces all objects, whereas that of the individual soul is the very opposite. Similar remarks apply to their powers of action. In the case of the Lord, action is caused by his mere existence

in the form of pure Consciousness, just as the action of burning is caused by the mere existence (in close proximity) of a substance like fire whose very nature is heat. And in the case of the Lord, action involves no change in Himself. It is like the 'action' of a king or of a magnet or of a light (which in each case induce change in others by their mere presence without special activity on their own part), whereas the action of the individual soul under transmigration is the opposite of this. Again, we have Vedic texts such as 'One should worship'[155] which show that the Lord is to be worshipped like a Teacher or a king, whereas the individual soul undergoing transmigration is the worshipper, like a pupil or a servant. And again, the Vedic texts show that the Lord is pure, by speaking of Him as beyond all evil, etc., whereas a text like 'He becomes pure through pure deeds'[156] shows that the individual soul undergoing transmigration is not pure....

Answer: But all this is wrong. For there are texts which denounce the habit of seeing distinctions, such as 'He does not know (aright) who thinks "He is one and I another"'[157].... And there are in fact thousands of texts which teach the fundamental identity of all.

As for the statement that the Lord and the soul undergoing transmigration must be different because the characteristics of their knowledge and power are different, we reply to that as follows. The objection cannot be sustained, as we refuse to admit the opponent's premises. There are no souls distinct from the Lord except as viewed through external adjuncts. We accept the one Lord, the Self of all beings, eternally free, as the sole reality. The Lord, the Self, eternally enlightened and free, is the basis of the individual personality, the latter marked by the limitations of the whole complex of false notions derived from the ego-feeling and the sense of possession associated with the sense-organs and the mind, etc. This complex, however, is a mere false appearance of eternal Consciousness, in which it appears as non-eternal, as different in nature from the Lord, as consisting of mind and its objects and nescience and its effects. As long as one is not severed from it (from the finite, individualized consciousness), one continues to have experience of transmigratory life. When one is severed from it, liberation supervenes.

The creatures, consisting in gods, ancestors and men, etc., are all found to undergo destruction in the end, like a coating of clay, and are accepted as being different from the Lord. Thus we accept the existence of the Lord as eternal changeless Consciousness, and we accept that his appearance in the form of empirical consciousness is (in some sense) different from Him, and we accept that the creatures, as perishable forms, are also different. But we do not accept any fourth category to include beings that are different from the Lord (and real). The expression used by the opponent (saying that the Lord and the individual souls were distinct) 'because they have different characteristics' represents an unfounded argument, because we only accept 'distinction' on the understanding that everything other than the Self is imagined through nescience, there being no other reality but the Lord.

Nor can you argue that we are attributing contradictory characteristics to the Lord or that He will, on our doctrine, be associated with pleasure and pain (as if He were Himself the transmigrant). For these are falsely attributed to Him by the people on account of an external conditioning factor. The sun is of the nature of constant light. But it is falsely supposed by the people to rise and set and to be the cause of day and night, simply because it is the condition (nimitta) whereby the world is sometimes manifest and sometimes not. The case with the Lord is similar. His nature is to be Consciousness and an eternal power. But humans are conditioned (by the external adjunct, the mind,) to enjoy now knowledge, now ignorance, now pleasure, now pain, now dreams. And pleasure and pain and the like are attributed anthropomorphically to the Lord, though his nature is the opposite of all that and He does not innately possess any such characteristics. False attribution is invariably based on one's own private experience. When the sky is overcast, one does not see the sun. One then goes on to say, erroneously, 'The sun is not shining now', although it is in fact shining elsewhere.... So it is that through nescience the state of transmigration is falsely imputed by the people to the Lord Himself, ever free, just as alternations of shining and not shining are falsely imputed to the sun (through the same cause). That the Lord is not really subject to transmigration is accepted on the authority of Vedic revelation, so there are no contradictions in our position.

What we have said above is also enough to refute the notion that each individual soul is also distinct (from each other individual soul) because its various experiences are distinct.[158] For there can be nothing to establish distinctions in their real core, where they are all without exception of the nature of subtle, all-pervading consciousness. And if the real nature of the individual soul were to undergo modification (into any particular characteristics) this would (involve impermanence and so) contradict the Vedic doctrine of its eternity. Moreover, philosophers do not admit distinctions in the state of liberation: and if distinctions were admitted as real at all they ought to be eternal (like everything else that is real). But the fact is that distinctions are only apprehended by those in the grip of nescience. When the latter is destroyed, they cease to have any validity. So our doctrine of the fundamental identity of all stands.... We speak of the 'bondage' of the Self and the 'liberation' of the Self (only) because bondage and liberation depend on the presence of the Self as consciousness for any reality whatever.[159]

❖

5. In the state of nescience, where the individual soul is blinded and does not distinguish himself from his instruments of action and knowledge (the senses and mental and physical powers), repeated births, in which he has the powers of agency and enjoyment, can proceed only by the permission (anujñā) of the highest Self, who, in the name of the Lord, dwells in all beings as their Witness, the controller of their actions and the source of their intelligence. And the liberation of the soul can only come through knowledge proceeding from his grace (anugraha).

How is this known? Because, says the Sūtra, there are passages in the Veda to this effect. True, the individual soul is prompted to act by his own psychological defects, and does himself possess the necessary prerequisites for action. And it must likewise be confessed that the co-operation of the Lord in such activities as tilling the soil is not generally recognized in the world. Nevertheless, it is definitely laid down in the Veda that the Lord is the cause of all actions in the world and hence the real agent, as such texts as the following show: 'Verily, him whom He wishes to raise above the worlds He causes to perform auspicious action' and 'He who, standing within the soul, controls the soul'.[160]

The Sūtra next goes on to rebut the suspicion that if the Lord is the cause of all action, He must be cruel and inclined to favouritism, and that the individual must incur the fruits of actions for which he is not himself responsible. The Lord only prompts action in relation to previous activity on the part of the individual soul, which already exists as merit and demerit. That is why the defects here suggested do not in fact apply. And it is only in relation to differences in the merits and demerits in the deeds of the various souls that He distributes different rewards as the results of their acts. Like the rain, He is not so much a cause as an occasion.[161] In worldly experience, we see that rain is a general occasion for the growth of various kinds of weeds and undergrowth and also of crops like rice and barley, each from their own particular seeds. The differences in juice, flowers, fruits and leaves could not develop without the rain on the one hand and the various seeds of each particular kind on the other. And in the same way the Lord distributes good and evil results to the individual souls in accordance with their previous deeds done on their own initiative.

Now, you might object that if the agency of the individual soul depended on the Lord, it would be wrong to speak of anything being in accordance with the soul's initiative. But the objection would be without force. The individual soul itself acts, even though it is dependent on the Lord for its power to do so. The Lord enables him to act now in accordance with his past deeds, and He enabled him to perform those past deeds on the basis of yet earlier ones; and you must accept this, as transmigration is admitted to be beginningless.[162]

But how is it known that the Lord causes the soul to act in accordance with its past deeds only (and not according to the arbitrary whims of the Lord Himself)? The Sūtra replies that this is known to be so because only thus will the Vedic texts giving injunctions and prohibitions be meaningful, and also for other additional reasons. For if the Lord exercised control over the deeds of the soul only in the way mentioned above, such injunctions and prohibitions as 'He who desires heaven should offer sacrifices' and 'One must not kill a Brahmin' would be meaningful, whereas if He exercised unconditional control they would be meaningless. It would be the Lord Himself to whom the injunctions and prohibitions would be directed, as the soul would be utterly under the control of another. Nor would there be anything to prevent the Lord granting evil to one who had done an enjoined act or good to one who had done a prohibited act, and on this basis the Veda would lose all authority. By 'other additional reasons' the Sūtra means that, if the Lord Himself did not depend on anything when He prompted the individual soul, effort even in secular matters would be useless and would not be duly conditioned by time, place and causal laws in the manner that it was earlier shown that it ought to be.[163] And there would be the other defects already mentioned (such as the soul's incurring the fruits of deeds that it did not perform).

The individual soul (says the next Sūtra) must be conceived as a part of the Lord, as a spark is a part of a fire.

'As a part' means 'as if' a part, for what is partless cannot have parts in the literal sense.

Well, but if the Lord is partless, why cannot the individual soul just be the Lord? It cannot, because there are texts which declare the two to be different. 'He is to be investigated, Him one should know'.... and 'He who, standing within the soul, controls the soul'[164] and other such texts would not be intelligible unless there were a difference between the Lord and the individual soul.

Now, you might think that these texts implying difference would fit in extremely well if the relation between the Lord and the individual soul were (a dualistic one) like that of master and servant. It is to forestall this idea that the Sūtra says, 'And also otherwise'. That is to say, it is not only because of the teaching implying difference between them that we know that the relation is that of part and whole; there is also the teaching that they are non-different. For some schools of the Atharva Veda speak of the Absolute (brahman) as comprising fishermen and gamblers in their 'Hymn to the Absolute',[165] in the words 'Fishermen are the Absolute, slaves are the Absolute, and so also, verily, are gamblers'.... The text says that all these, too, are the Absolute, and by singling out unfortunate folk teaches that all souls whatever who have come into the complex of body, mind and senses, arising from name and form, are the Absolute.... And consciousness is not different in the individual soul and the Lord, just as heat is identical in fire and sparks. Thus we know that the individual soul is a part of the Lord because we hear of it in the Veda as being different and also as being non-different from the Lord....

But what about the opinion mentioned above (tentatively) that in the world the Lord-and-his-subject relation was only found (subsisting between two separate entities), as in the case of master-and-servant, (and not between two things which are identical). It is true that this holds in regard to secular experience. But we know from the Veda that there can be both a part-and-whole relation and a Lord-and-subject relation. There is nothing actually to contradict the idea that the Lord associated with his supremely majestic adjunct rules over the individual souls with their humble adjunct (as long as it is remembered that the ruler-and-ruled relation applies to the external adjuncts, while the Lord and the soul remain identical in their true essence).

Objection: If one were really to admit that the individual soul was a part of the Lord, then the Lord, as the whole, would undergo pain along with the pain undergone by the part in the course of the transmigratory experience of the latter. It would be like the example in ordinary experience where the person, Devadatta, as the whole, undergoes the pain undergone by some part of his body, say the hand or the foot. So it would follow that anyone who attained to the state of the Lord would experience far more pain than he is experiencing now. People would therefore prefer to stay in their previous condition of transmigratory life, and the theory would undermine the ideal of liberation through right vision.

Answer: We do not admit that the Lord experiences pain in the way that the individual soul does in the course of transmigratory life. Because the individual soul is permeated by nescience, it becomes identified in practice with the body and the rest of the psycho-physical organism. And in this condition it accepts as its own the experience of pain suggested in the form of 'It is I who am the sufferer' in regard to pains arising from the body. But the supreme Lord neither identifies Himself with the body nor accepts pain. Even in the case of the individual soul, experience of pain is not real in the highest sense, but arises from the error of failing to distinguish himself from the body and sense-organs and other external adjuncts, which are composed of name and form, which latter are in turn but figments of nescience.[166] The soul experiences the pain arising from cuts and burns in its body through identifying itself with them in error. And it experiences the pains of sons and friends and the like in the same way, through identifying itself with them in error, cleaving to son and friend with cloying affection and verily imagining himself to be them.

From this we arrive at the following generalization: all experience of pain is based on false identification. And we arrive at the same result from a consideration of negative instances. Imagine, for example, that there is a large company consisting partly of family persons who have some friends, and who feel themselves connected to their relatives and friends by ties of supposed identification, and that there are also others in the party (monks and renunciates, etc.,) who are not so affected. And suppose, further, that announcements are made to the company that such and such a son and such and such a friend are dead. In that case, only those who accept that they have sons or friends will feel grief, not those, such as wandering monks and others, who do not have such feelings. When right vision is seen to work to the advantage even of men of this world (in minimizing pain), how much more will this be true in the case of one who has gone beyond the realm of objects and sees nothing but his own Self, of the nature of eternal pure Consciousness. So it is not right to say that our view would mean that right knowledge was of no value.

The Sūtra illustrates this by saying, 'The Supreme does not (suffer) in this way, as it is like light, etc.' Consider the light of either the sun or the moon diffused through the ether. When it comes into contact with external objects like the fingers of the hand, then whenever the latter are stretched or crooked the light will appear to be affected without actually being affected. Similarly, the ether will appear to move when pots and the like (which appear to enclose portions of it) are carried about, but it will not actually do so. Similarly, when a vessel of water is shaken, the reflection of the sun will shake, while the sun, the original to which that reflection belongs, will not shake. And in the same way, when the ray or part, known as the individual soul, which is delimited only by external adjuncts like the mind and which is a creation of nescience, undergoes pain, the Lord, to whom that ray or part belongs, will not undergo pain.... And thus it is that such upanishadic texts as 'That thou art'[167] negate the individuality of the individual soul, since its nature as such is conditioned by nescience, and teach that it is really the Absolute. So it cannot be said that the supreme Self undergoes any pain on account of the pain undergone by the individual soul....

(As for the view that the individual soul is a part of the Lord because He is known to be both different and non-different from Him), we could only accept this if the Veda were really concerned with teaching both the difference and the non-difference of the individual soul from the Lord on an equal footing. But the fact is that it is only concerned with teaching the non-difference of the individual soul from the Lord, as man accomplishes his true ends by realizing that the Self (i.e. his true Self) and the Absolute are one.[168] In so far as it teaches difference it merely restates what the soul already thinks naturally.[169] And we have already said that the individual soul cannot literally be a part of the partless Absolute. Therefore it is but right to say that it is the supreme principle itself, the one inner Self in all beings, which becomes the individual soul through phenomenal conditioning.[170]

❖

6. How is it that the Veda can say, 'The Self is to be sought',[171] and the Smṛti can say, 'There is no greater gain than that of the Self',[172] when you have said that the one who gains cannot himself be the one who is gained? True, we reply, this seems like a difficulty. But what has happened is that the not-self, such as the body and its organs, has generally come to be seen as the Self, and this comes about through ignorance of the true nature of the Self, which never really falls from that true nature. And from the standpoint of the 'self' thus constituted by the body and its organs it is but right to speak of the true Self as something distinct, as not properly investigated into and requiring investigation, as not yet heard about and requiring to be heard about, as not yet cogitated over and requiring to be cogitated over, as not yet understood and requiring to be understood, etc.

And yet from the standpoint of the ultimate truth such texts as 'There is no other Seer but He'[173] deny that there is any seer or hearer other than the omniscient supreme Lord. But the supreme Lord is different from the embodied soul, the agent and enjoyer called the self conditioned by the intellect (vijñāna-ātman).[174] The case is parallel with that of the mass hypnotist's magic display, where the magician on the ground, the real figure, is different from his double, appearing with sword and shield, having climbed up into the sky on a rope.[175] Or again, the case is parallel with that of the universal ether, which, itself untouched by an external adjunct, is different from that of the 'pot-ether' apparently enclosed within an external adjunct (the pot).[176]

❖

7. On the assumption that the individual soul attained to the Absolute (on liberation), the individual soul, as that which did the attaining would have to be either a part of, or a modification of, or different from the Absolute, that to which it attained. For if it were *absolutely* identical there could be no question of attaining.

What follows from our contention? If the soul constituted a particular part of the Absolute, that part would always be present within the Absolute, and hence there could be no question of the soul attaining the Absolute on this supposition either. And the whole conception of being a part of the Absolute is incorrect anyway, as the Absolute is known to be partless. And the assumption that the individual soul is a modification of the Absolute suffers from similar defects. For a modification is likewise always present within that of which it is a modification.[177] The pot cannot give up its nature as clay and still continue to exist: if it did give it up, it would cease to exist. Further, if the individual soul were taken to be either a modification or a part of the Absolute, it would not be able to enter transmigratory life, as the Absolute, that of which it was a modification or part, is perfectly motionless.

So we are driven back to supposing that the individual soul is different from the Absolute. If this be the case, the soul must be either atomic or all-pervading or of middle size. If it were all-pervasive, it could not attain to anything. If it were of middling size, it (would be composed of parts and so) could not be eternal. If it were atomic, (it could very well be eternal but) the fact that we have sensations all over the body would be inexplicable. Moreover, we have refuted the notions that it could be atomic or of middle size in detail above.[178] And if the individual soul were really different from the supreme Self, that would be in contradiction with such texts as 'That thou art'.[179] This last difficulty also applies to the contention that the individual soul is either a modification or a part of the Absolute. Nor can you retort that the modification and the part are non-different from the original substance and the whole respectively, (for this is a mere play with words) since they cannot be totally identical with them. All these views (of the relationship between the individual soul and the Absolute) involve the impossibility of liberation. For they imply that the transmigrant's nature as transmigrant never ceases, or, if it does cease, involves the destruction of the transmigrant in his true and essential nature. They come to this result because they do not admit that the ultimate Self of man is (identical with) the Absolute (brahman).[180]

❖

8. Do we mean that the individual soul and the Lord have no common element whatever? No, we do not. A common nature exists, but is hidden by the veil of nescience and the other defects. This common nature, being hidden, manifests through the grace of the supreme Lord in the case of one or two perfect souls only, those who meditate on the Lord and who make great efforts to throw off their ignorance. In their case the grace of the supreme Lord operates like medicine operating to restore vision that has become obscured by an eye-disease. But the essential identity with the Lord, which all beings in fact possess, does not manifest to them all naturally.

Why is this so? Because, as the author of the Sūtras puts it, the bondage and liberation of the soul come from the Lord; when the true nature of the Lord is not known there is bondage, when it is known there is liberation.[181]

❖

9. *Objection:* And here one might suppose that the word 'Self' could not refer to the 'I' of the hearer. For that which has divine qualities like freedom from all contact with evil cannot be conceived as having the opposite nature, and neither can that which is of the opposite nature be conceived as having divine qualities like freedom from all touch of evil....

Answer: Against this contention we (Advaitins) maintain that the supreme Lord, verily, is the Self of the one undergoing transmigration. For, to mention one example, the Jābālas, in speaking of the supreme Lord, maintain that He is the Self of the individual soul, as expressed in their text, 'O holy deity! I, verily, am one with Thee, and Thou, O Lord, art one with me'....[182]

What was said about this being only a theme for symbolic meditation on the model of a meditation on an image of Viṣṇu (where it is clear that the image only represents Viṣṇu and that Viṣṇu is not limited to the image) was wrong. For it would mean that all texts that taught identity would have to be interpreted as figurative (even when the literal sense would not have been contradictory). And it is also wrong because the form of the texts in which identity is taught is different from that of those giving symbolic meditations. When a symbolic meditation is intended, the identity-statement only occurs once, as, for example, 'The mind is the Absolute' or 'The sun is the Absolute'.[183] But in the texts we are considering now we find a double statement of identity in the form 'Thou art one with me and I am one with Thee'. Hence the form of the texts in which the identity of the soul with the Lord is taught is different from the form of those in which symbolic meditations are given.

Moreover, there are texts denying the existence of any differences anywhere. Many a text decries the vision of difference in general, such as 'He goes from death to death who sees the appearance of variety here' and 'Everything rejects him who thinks of everything as other than the Self'.[184]

It was also said that there cannot be identity of nature between things that have contradictory qualities. But this does not affect our position. For they can very well have contradictory qualities if the latter are illusory (mithyā). As for the statement that the doctrine of the identity of the Lord with the individual soul would imply the non-existence of the Lord (as such), that was just wrong. For we have the authority of the Veda to show that the Lord does exist, and we do not understand the doctrine of his identity with the individual soul in the way that the opponent supposed. For our view is not that the Veda teaches that the Lord is identical with the one who undergoes transmigration (as such). What we hold the Vedic doctrine to be is that the one who is undergoing transmigration finds himself identical with the Lord when he throws off his nature as transmigrant. This being so, the Lord, one without a second, can very well have the divine qualities such as freedom from all contact with evil, and the notion that the soul is characterized by the opposite qualities is revealed as illusory.

It was also said that the doctrine of the identity of the individual soul and the Lord would undermine the utility of the Veda because there would then be no one who needed it, and that it also stood in contradiction with immediate perception. But both these points are also wrong. For we admit that the soul is subject to the evils of transmigration before enlightenment, while perception and other empirical means of knowledge pertain only to this (pre-enlightenment) realm. For there are texts, such as 'But where all this has become his own Self, what could he see and with what?',[185] which show that on enlightenment perception and the other means of empirical knowledge cease. Nor can you object against us that if perception and the other empirical means of knowledge fall away, the Veda, as an authoritative means of knowledge, falls away with them. For this is precisely our doctrine. We base our doctrine that the Veda itself disappears at enlightenment on the authority of the passage which begins 'Where the father is no father' and goes on later to say 'and the Vedas are no Vedas'.[186]

If you now ask, 'To whom, then, does this absence of enlightenment pertain?' we reply that it pertains to you who are asking the question. And if you then object, 'But am I not declared in the Veda to be the Lord?' we reply that if you are awake to this then (you will see that in truth) there is no absence of enlightenment for anyone.

This line of reasoning has also silenced those who try to raise the objection that the Self becomes associated with a second (i.e. with duality) if we admit nescience,[187] and that this contradicts the Vedic statements that it is one without a second. So one should apply one's mind to the idea that the Lord is verily one's own Self.[188]

❖

NOTES TO CHAPTER VIII

References to Extracts are in bold type

(List of abbreviations, pp 211-213; Bibliography, pp 214-232)

1 A definition of this term has been given above, Vol.II, Chap.V, section 1, introduction.

2 Sac, M.R.V., 230f.

3 Deutsch, 53. Cp. below, section 2, Extract 11.

4 Ghate, 52-56.

5 One might cite, apart from Ghate, Radhakrishnan I.P. Vol.II, 440; Thibaut Vol.I, Intro., livff.; Belvalkar, *Vedanta Philosophy*, 160; Gonda, *Inleiding*, 230; Grousset Vol.II, 303; Sāṅkṛtyāyana, 677; Strauss, 233f.; von Glasenapp, *Einführung*, 182f.

6 Bṛhad. IV.v.13.

7 Chānd. VIII.xii.4.

8 Bṛhad. IV.iii.23.

9 B.S.Bh. II.iii.18.

10 Śvet. III.8.

11 Chānd. VI.viii.1.

12 Chānd. VI.ix.2.

13 B.S.Bh. II.iii.30-31.

14 In dreamless sleep the body is non-conscious and indifferent to being pushed. If there can be awakening through pushing of the body in dreamless sleep, this points to the presence within the body of an experiencer who is other than the body.

15 Bṛhad. Bh. II.i.15.

16 Ait. Bh. I.iii.12.

17 Because the earth-element contains the other four. Cp. above, Vol.II, Chap.VI, section 3, Extracts 4-7. Thus all five elements enter into the constitution of the body of man, which explains, for instance, how his sense-organs are able to apprehend the five elements in sense-perception, on the principle that like knows like.

18 See Manu Smṛti, II.29ff.

19 *Ibid.* II.36ff.

20 U.S. (prose) 20-23.

21 Chānd. VI.xi.3.

22 Bṛhad. IV.iii.8.

23 B.S.Bh. II.iii.16.

24 Śvet. VI.11.

25 Bṛhad. IV.iv.5. In this text, 'mano-maya, etc.' literally mean 'made up of mind, etc.' The Self is not literally 'made up of mind', so Śaṅkara quotes a phrase from secular speech to show that the suffix '-maya' can be used figuratively to mean 'identified with' — strī-maya, identified with women.

26 Bṛhad. IV.v.14 (Mādhyandina recension).

27 B.S.Bh. II.iii.17.

28 The Upanishad text has compared the Absolute to an ocean of water and the individual soul to a lump of salt that first forms in it and later redissolves without trace.

29 Bṛhad. Bh. II.iv.12.

30 They only serve the purposes of the conscious being who put them together in order to have a house.

31 The Teacher means that in the case of the master and servant we are speaking about the complex of the Self and the illusory

adjuncts forming the individual personality. In this situation, the illusory elements (body and mind, etc.,) belonging to the two personalities can be of service to each other mutually. Cp. above, Vol.II, Chap.V, section 3, Extract 7.

32 I.e. I was thinking of your real Self with consciousness for its essential property.

33 U.S. (prose) 64-74.

34 In Śaṅkara, the term ābhāsa can mean either 'reflection' or 'illusory appearance' according to the context. Mayeda, W.Z.K.S.O., 1968/9, 33.

35 A reference to the three guṇas.

36 **Chānd. Bh. VI.iii.2.** The Vedic quotation was from Chānd. VI.i.4.

37 The Veda starts by accommodating its teaching to the standpoint of the unenlightened man. From that standpoint empirical knowledge is a fact and the Veda affirms that the real knower is the Self.

38 Praśna Bh. IV.9.

39 Mayeda quotes Manu Smṛti, IV.130, Yājñavalkya Smṛti, I.152. The later commentator on the B.S., Vallabhācārya, claims, at his B.S.Bh. II.iii.50, that the word 'ābhāsa' in the Sūtra does not mean something totally unreal, referring to the pre-Śaṅkara Vṛttikāra (commentator). This would point to a belief amongst certain Vedantins before Śaṅkara's day that the ābhāsa was in some sense a reality. The term also means a shadow, and so shade; hence the idea of 'coolness'.

40 E.g. At Chānd. VIII.xiii.1. Rāhu is the eclipse personified as a monster that devours the sun and moon. It must be remembered in what follows that, as was seen in the previous note, Sanskrit uses the same words for 'shadow' and 'reflection'.

41 This has been traced to the second and third verses of the Golapāda of Ārya Bhaṭṭa (sixth century AD or earlier). The same writer, whose view that the earth spun round was later rejected, explained the apparent motion of the stars by the example of the optical illusions of a traveller moving in a boat, who sees relative motion amongst the objects on the bank even where it does not exist. Upādhyāya, R., 531, also Renou and Filliozat II, 88. Śaṅkara uses the same example for his purposes at U.S. (verse) V.2-4.

42 E.g. If a sentence is authoritative as a command, it cannot be authoritative as a statement of fact at the same time. The exegetical principle invoked is that of 'Ekavākyatā', for which see Keith, *Mīmāṃsā*, 82.

43 The view of Kumārila.

44 U.S. (verse) XVIII.32-50.

45 See Vol.IV, Chap.XI, section 3, below. According to Śaṅkara, the Sāṅkhyas did not admit a reflection of consciousness in their theory of the individual soul, being content with the mere theory of 'proximity', sānnidhya. Hence they could not bridge the gap between the soul as pure consciousness (puruṣa) and Nature.

46 According to the Sāṅkhya system, the soul as pure consciousness does not have any of the characteristics of Nature such as change, etc. See Vol.IV, Chap.XI, section 4, below.

47 The commentator produces verse 11 of the Brahma Bindu or Amṛta Bindu Upanishad. This is a comparatively late work, though possibly quoted by Śaṅkara at B.S.Bh. III.ii.18 *ad fin.* The fact is that the need for a reflection theory had by no means dawned on the sages of the classical Upanishads, though Śaṅkara interpreted their texts as *implying* the need to assume one, as the next Extract will show.

48 Śaṅkara is on firm ground here, as reflection imagery was

current in Hindu religious teaching long before his day. The poet Kālidāsa (*Raghuvaṃśa* X.65) uses the image of the moon reflected in different water-pots to show how the one Viṣṇu, though indivisible, was born in four different forms in the wombs of three wives of Daśaratha.

49 One is dependent on one's knowledge of the Self to know that the reflection is in fact a reflection of the Self. And one is dependent on one's knowledge that the reflection is a reflection of the Self to know the Self. One cannot, therefore, establish the existence of the Self without tacitly assuming in advance the existence of that which one wishes to prove. In the case of the mirror, however, this is not so, as knowledge of the existence of the mirror is available independently of knowledge of the reflection.

50 Dream is a special case for the clear apprehension of the Self as Witness. For there subsequent waking experience shows that there are no external objects, so it is especially clear (to later introspection) that the mental ideas were themselves objects for a Witness. B.S.Bh. III.ii.4, trans. Gambhīrānanda, 593; Bṛhad. Bh. IV.iii.9, trans. Mādhavānanda, 442. See also below, Chap.IX, section 2. **U.S. (verse) XVIII.111-117.**

51 **B.S.Bh. II.iii.50.**

52 Śaṅkara speaks of a 'part' or 'ray' in commenting on this famous Gītā verse, but he never admitted that the Self had parts from the standpoint of the highest truth. See the following note.

53 If a thing has parts, these parts must have been brought together at some point in time, and at some other point in time they are bound to disintegrate.

54 **Bh.G.Bh. XV.7.**

55 All the great elements forming the world proceed from the ether, and hence all objects composed of them do likewise.

56 The organism as here understood includes the subtle body,

which outlasts any given physical body and transmigrates. Hence final dissolution only takes place with enlightenment, not with the death of the physical body if enlightenment has not been achieved.

57 G.K.Bh. III.3 and 4.

58 Bṛhad. IV.iv.22.

59 M.Bh. XII.232.9.

60 See Vol.IV, Chap.XI, section 6, below.

61 B.S.Bh. II.iii.29.

62 Section 1, Extract 5, above.

63 See Vol.V, Chap.XII, section 1, below.

64 B.S.Bh. II.iv.7, IV.ii.9.

65 See Vol.II, Chap.VI, section 4, Extract 8.

66 This was the standard doctrine of the time, deriving from Nyāya Sūtra II.i.62-73. Mayeda W.Z.K.S.O., 1968/9, 224.

67 Cp. Hacker, *Upadeshasāhasrī*, 50, note 27.

68 T.B.V. II.234, quoted Sac, M.V., 342.

69 Sac, *ibid.*, 525.

70 Bṛhad. Bh. II.iv.11.

71 Bṛhad. Bh. I.v.3.

72 The mind is taken as embracing both knowledge and will. If a distinction between manas and buddhi is made (as at Bh.G.Bh. V.13, trans. A.M. Śāstrī, 167), then it is the same organ that is called manas when alternative notions or resolutions are still in play (the state of doubt or indecision), and buddhi when there is determinate knowledge or fixed resolution (the state of decision). It is called citta in so far as it engages in memory

and pleasure-pain feeling, and ahaṅkāra in so far as its states are accompanied by a feeling of individuality.

73 Bṛhad. I.v.3. **B.S.Bh. II.iv.6.**

74 Both terms, buddhi and vijñāna, originally meant knowledge or consciousness in a wide sense, but gradually acquired an additional specialized or technical meaning, more especially associated with buddhi, of determinate knowledge or fixed resolution. Cp. Johnston, 55, footnote.

75 Ahaṅkāra is omitted here. For Śaṅkara it was not so much a special faculty or mode of the mind as the sense of 'I' (understood as an individual) that accompanies all our activities. See Śaṅkara's B.S.Bh. II.iii.38.

76 **B.S.Bh. II.iii.32.**

77 Chānd. VIII.xii.5.

78 **Chānd. Bh. VI.v.1.**

79 The sense of smell and its object, odour, are made up of the special quality of the earth-element, viz. odour. The tongue, as an organ of taste, together with tastes themselves, proceeds from the special quality of the water-element. Sight and colour proceed from light, the quality of the fire-element. The sense of touch and its objects proceed from the special quality of the wind-element. The sense of hearing and sound proceed from the special quality of the ether. Cp. M.Bh. XII.202.20 (G.P. Ed. Vol.III, 538); also Extract 1, present section.

80 For the Vaiśeṣika, pleasure and pain were qualities of the soul. For the Sāṅkhya and Vedantin they were qualities of the antaḥkaraṇa, which was distinct from the soul, and its mere external adjunct, while the soul, as pure Consciousness, was ever free from them.

81 Cp. Sureśvara, N.Sid. II.80.

82 The eye can also be seen by others: in any case the point being made is that whereas the sense-organs are substances composed of parts, the Self is not, and the Self could never be subject and object of the same act. **U.S. verse XVI.1-10.**

83 This account tallies with that of the next Extract, except for the wider range of functions given to udāna in the passage below. Another special function of udāna in dreamless sleep is mentioned at Praśna Bh. IV.4.

84 Bṛhad. I.iii.22.

85 **B.S.Bh. II.iv.12-13.**

86 The word 'prāṇa' has the prefix 'pra' meaning forwards. Cp. 'pro' in Greek and Latin, German 'vor' and English 'fore', 'forwards'.

87 Although the names of the five subdivisions of the Vital Energy in the body are the same in the Sāṅkhya system according to the Y.D. Commentary on Īśvara Kṛṣṇa's Sāṅkhya Kārikā 29, the functions are differently attributed in the two systems. Cp. Frauwallner, G.I.P., Vol.I, 367f. **Bṛhad. Bh. I.v.3.**

88 Ait. I.ii.4.

89 *Ibid.*

90 Chānd. III.xviii.3.

91 Bṛhad. I.iii.12, cp. Bṛhad. I.v.11.

92 Cp. Chānd. VIII.xii.3, 'As an animal is attached to a cart, so is the Vital Energy attached to the body'.

93 Chānd. VIII.xii.4.

94 If you continue to recognize yourself as the same person, you must be the same person recognizing yourself.

95 Bṛhad. I.v.20. **B.S.Bh. II.iv.14-16.**

96 Śvet. III.19, Śvet. III.4. **Chānd. Bh. V.i.15.**

97 Taitt. II.5.

98 The immediate context is meditation on the Absolute as associated with various forms: it is only the discipline as a whole that leads on to a discriminatory knowledge of the supreme Self. The supreme Self does not itself form the subject of the various stages of meditation.

99 According to Sac's commentary, identification with the bliss self implies rising above the sense of individual agency, while remaining attached to that of individual 'enjoyerhood'. Thus interpreted, it might be compared with the state of aesthetic contemplation.

100 See Taitt. II.7, Bṛhad. IV.iii.32, Taitt. II.8. **Taitt. Bh. II.2-5 (selected).**

101 Seventeen-fold = 5 sense organs + 5 organs of action + 5 modifications of the Vital Energy + manas and buddhi. All these factors have already been explained earlier in the section.

102 In the earlier belief, these luminous rays of different colour were connected with luminous rays proceeding from the sun. Frauwallner, G.I.P., Vol.I, 61.

103 **Bṛhad. Bh. IV.iii.20.**

104 Ś.B. VIII.vii.2.11. **B.S.Bh. IV.ii.9-11.**

105 The 'causal' body of the Self is probably to be defined as 'causal nescience, called the Unmanifest...Nature, the Cause, Nescience, the seed of desire and action', in accordance with Īśa Bh. 12. Cp. B.S.Bh. I.iv.2. But it is noteworthy that when the Īśa verse now under comment is explained at U.S. (verse) IV.10, the purity of the Self is only made the ground for excluding any subtle body. There is no mention of a 'causal' body at all. We hear much about the causal body from later Advaita authors, but it is essentially a post-Śaṅkara conception. **Īśa Bh. 8.**

106 I.e. in dreamless sleep.

107 samprasāda, Bṛhad. IV.iii.15.

108 At Bṛhad. IV.iii.12 and II.i.18, cp. B.S. II.iii.34 and 35.

109 B.S.Bh. II.iii.40.

110 Reflected light. See section 3, Extract 6, below.

111 U.S. (verse) XVI.20-22.

112 See Hacker, *Vedanta Studien* I, esp. 242-246.

113 See above, section 2, Extract 1.

114 A red-hot iron will brand skin. We speak loosely of 'branding with the iron'. But reflective analysis shows that the iron is not the real agent in the burning. That 'through which' the iron burns is fire, which is different from iron.

115 Kaṭha Bh. II.i.3.

116 The meaning of the phrase 'through which' varies according to circumstances. In the previous Extract, the Self was that 'by virtue of which' the instruments are able to operate, that on which they depend for light. In the present Extract, the chief instrument 'through which' the Self enjoys empirical knowledge cannot be that which has knowledge, as an instrument is what exists for the sake of another.

117 The cow and horse and 'Bravo' are examples taken from the text under comment, Ait. I.ii.2 and 3.

118 Ait. Āraṇyaka II.i.3, II.i.7 and II.iv.1. (Ed. Keith, 102, 106 and 118.) Cp. Ait. Upan. I.i.4.

119 Kauṣītaki III.6.

120 Bṛhad. I.v.3 and III.ix.20.

121 Kauṣītaki III.3.

122 At Bh.G.Bh. VII.11 Śaṅkara opposes this to rāga (= attachment to what one already has).

123 The various qualities are in fact only states of mind, but are attributed figuratively to Consciousness, since mind is the instrument through which Consciousness enters into empirical experience.

124 Ait. Bh. III.i.1-2.

125 On prājña, see also Chap. IX, sections 2 and 3, below.

126 When a snake emerges from its hole into the sunlight, the sun does not 'illumine' it by any new act. Similarly, the Self does not actively illumine the cognitions. They merely pass into its light.

127 Taitt. II.1.

128 On the meaning of words being restricted to genus, quality, action and relation, cp. above Vol.1, Chap.III, section 3, Extract 1.

129 U.S. (verse) XV.11-34.

130 U.S. (verse) XIV.1-8.

131 U.S. (verse) XVIII.153-157.

132 The eclipse, personified as a monster who devours the sun or moon. Cp. Chānd. VIII.xiii.1.

133 Bṛhad. I.v.3.

134 I.e. they identify themselves initially with the intellect and then later with the sense-organs, body and external possessions through that.

135 Here Śaṅkara distinguishes between intellect (buddhi) as the higher function which attains fixity and certitude in will and knowledge, and the lower mind (manas) as the same principle in a state of fluctuation and doubt.

136 A play on words between puruṣa and pūrṇa.

137 They are objects for consciousness and so cannot themselves supply it.

138 Bṛhad. IV.iv.5.

139 Bṛhad. Bh. IV.iii.7.

140 In the previous Sūtra the opinion of the Teacher, Auḍulomi, has been mentioned, according to whom Vedic texts speaking of the 'passage' of the released soul from the bodily conditions to unity with the supreme Self implied a certain distinction between the soul and the supreme Self.

141 In the B.S.Bh. vijñāna-ātman = jīva. See Deussen, *System*, footnote 82. At Praśna IV.9 and IV.11 it means the highest Self.

142 Chānd. VI.iii.2.

143 The promise at Bṛhad. II.iv.5, 'when the Self is known, all is known'. On Āśmarathya, cp. B.S.Bh. I.iv.20.

144 Chānd. VI.viii.7, etc.

145 Cp. Kena II.4.

146 Bṛhad. IV.v.13.

147 Bṛhad. IV.v.14. The presence of the final clause (mātrā-asaṃsargas tv asya bhavati) shows that the Mādhyandina recension is being followed. (Deussen) So the phrase is not found, for instance, in Radhakrishnan's *The Principal Upanishads*, 285.

148 Bṛhad. II.iv.13.

149 B.S.Bh. I.iv.22.

150 Ait. I.1, Chānd. VI.ii.3, etc.

151 B.S.Bh. I.i.5.

152 All the positions retailed in the opening stages of the present argument are tentative. The Advaitin does not show his hand until a considerably later stage.

153 This may be seen as an affirmation of the Law of Identity.

154 Bṛhad. Bh. II.i.20.

155 Bṛhad. I.iv.7. Upāsīta can mean either 'worship'or 'meditate on'.

156 Bṛhad. III.ii.13.

157 Bṛhad. I.iv.10.

158 The Sāṅkhyas adopted this line of reasoning probably under Vaiśeṣika influence. Frauwallner, G.I.P., I, 322f.

159 Bondage and liberation consist in ignorance of the Self followed by removal of that ignorance. These two appearances do not affect the nature of the Self at all. **Kena (Vākya) Bh. III.1.**

160 Kauṣītaki III.8 and Bṛhad. III.vii.22.

161 Malebranche uses the same simile in a similar context. Cp. Cresson, 120.

162 If transmigration were not beginningless, the original bias to some line of action would have had to have been given by the Lord, who would thus become responsible altogether for the soul's actions and so open to the charge of cruelty and favouritism, etc.

163 B.S.Bh. II.iii.37.

164 Chānd. VIII.vii.1 and Bṛhad. III.vii.27.

165 Brahma Sūkta VIII.9. The text has been located in the Paippalāda Śākhā Saṃhitā of the Kashmīrī Atharva Veda. See Jośī, T.L., *Vaidika Saṃskṛti*, 68, and (same author) *Dharma Kośa Upaniṣat Kāṇḍa*, 252. Do we have evidence here for associating Śaṅkara with Kashmir? If so, it might have a

bearing on the possible authenticity of the Mānasollāsa commentary attributed to his pupil Sureśvara on the Dakṣiṇāmūrti Stotra — the commentary shows the influence of Kashmiri Shaivism.

166 Śaṅkara did not regard nescience as constituting the material cause of the world, though it came to be so regarded among the later writers of his school. For him, the body, etc., are composed of name and form. Name-and-form is their material cause and is imagined through nescience.

167 Chānd. VI. viii.7.

168 Only those texts of the Veda are authoritative on matters of fact which convey fruitful knowledge not otherwise accessible.

169 A restatement of this kind cannot be part of the Veda's essential message, as the latter exists to teach something new. The Veda may occasionally restate what the soul already thinks about its own nature in the natural course, but only as part of its method of communicating the truth by stages. Such passages must be rejected as false from the standpoint of the highest truth.

170 From B.S.Bh. II.iii.41-47.

171 Chānd. VIII.vii.1.

172 Appears at Āpastamba Sūtra Praśna 1, Paṭala 8, 2.

173 Bṛhad. III.vii.23.

174 I.e. the individual soul, cp. Note 141 above.

175 On the Indian rope trick, cp. above Vol.II, Chap.V, section 5, Extract 12.

176 B.S.Bh. I.i.17.

177 So that it cannot 'attain' it.

178 A small part of the argumentation has been reproduced at section 1, Extract 17, above.

179 Chānd.VI.viii.7.

180 B.S.Bh. IV.iii.14.

181 B.S.Bh. III.ii.5.

182 This verse appears as Varāha Upanishad II.34 at Rāghorām, 476, but does not appear in modern recensions of the Jābāla Upanishad. Śaṅkara apparently knew the texts of the Jābālas in a fuller form than that of the Jābāla Upanishad as it has come down to us.

183 Chānd. III.viii.1 and III.ix.1.

184 Bṛhad. IV.iv.19, IV.v.7.

185 Bṛhad. II.iv.14.

186 Bṛhad. IV.iii.22.

187 The reference is to Kumārila, cp. above Vol.I, 37f.

188 B.S.Bh. IV.i.3.

CHAPTER IX

THE 'STATES' OF THE SOUL AND THEIR TRANSCENDENCE

1. Dream

The present chapter will complete the exposition of the positive side of Śaṅkara's theoretical teaching, so far as it can be separated from his practical teaching. Only the criticism of erroneous views remains, and this will be taken as part of his practical teaching in the sense that it is designed to protect the pupil from what might hinder him from carrying the practical teaching out. Hence it will be reserved for the fourth volume. Before embarking on this last chapter of the present volume, let us glance back briefly and take stock of the ground covered in the Source-Book so far.

After reviewing some of the historical antecedents to Śaṅkara's teaching in the opening chapter of Volume I, we saw in Chapter II that he taught that man's sufferings and limitations are due solely to his ignorance of his own true nature as infinite Spirit. We saw in Chapter III that even in the state of spiritual ignorance he is already in some sense aware of himself as infinite Spirit, but that this knowledge has become overlaid with a covering of false knowledge that has to be negated through the assimilation of the traditional wisdom. Since the latter is transmitted through words, which are intelligible only in the domain of plurality, it has to begin with positive affirmations which serve to divert the mind of the student from its natural preoccupation with what is spiritually valueless, affirmations which are false in themselves and have to be transcended through subsequent negation.

(IX. 1) THE 'STATES' OF THE SOUL

Chapter IV dealt with the highest and most abstract forms of affirmation of the Absolute. Chapter V, which marks the transition to Volume II, dealt with the Absolute endowed with personal attributes and conceived as the Creator and Controller of the world. Chapter VI dealt with the upanishadic doctrine of the nature of the world and of the subordinate deities presiding over its manifestation. And then in Chapter VII all this affirmative teaching was swept aside from a higher standpoint, that of the negation of all finitude and limitation.

A similar pattern is now being followed in the theoretical account of the nature of the human soul being developed in the present (third) volume. The different sections of Chapter VIII showed how the real element in the soul was the light of Consciousness, the eternal, immortal, infinite Spirit, although in the state of nescience this light becomes identified with the body and mind and other organs and powers of the individual, so that he comes to think of himself as limited, suffering and mortal. In the present chapter, however, the element of negation will eventually reappear. The first two sections will give accounts of the dream and dreamless sleep states of the soul respectively. But the third and final section will show that neither of these states affect the soul in its true nature at all. In its true nature, the soul inhabits neither the realm of waking experience nor that of dream-experience nor even that of dreamless sleep, but a fourth (turīya or turya) realm, which is not separate from the others, and is only called 'the Fourth' from the standpoint of ignorance, to contrast it with the other three, which it transcends and negates.

Thus if Śaṅkara's teaching is taken out of the commentaries in which it is embedded and re-arranged in more systematic form, his texts dealing with the nature of the soul can very well be represented as falling under the same pattern as those dealing with the world of Nature. The world is first admitted to exist as a fact of experience, and accounts of its 'creation' are reproduced from the

Vedic texts. But since the world is evidently not self-sufficient, it can be treated as a kind of finger pointing to a self-sufficient principle beyond, its ground. This self-existent principle is conceived as related to the world in various ways, and described as its Projector, Controller, Support and Witness. Finally negative texts are introduced which point to a higher standpoint, viewed from which the world is robbed of all its solidity, and the Absolute of all its finite characteristics. Similarly, the experiences of the individual soul in the realm of limitation are at first taken at their face value, though it is also shown that they point to the presence of a self-luminous and transcendent Witness within. But we shall see in the last section of the present chapter that reflection on the implications of the continual passage from dreamless sleep to waking and back to dream and dreamless sleep prepares the way for the introduction of a higher standpoint, viewed from which the three states have no reality whatever, and only the timeless Spirit, the eternal Witness, exists. Thus Śaṅkara's teaching can be represented as repeating on a more elaborate scale the old upanishadic process of enquiry into Brahman as the principle behind the world, and into Ātman as the principle behind the soul, leading to the eventual identification of the two in the realm which transcends all plurality.

The first Extract in the present section vindicates the interpretation just suggested in so far as it claims that the doctrine of the three states of the soul (waking, dream and dreamless sleep) is only introduced in the Upanishads to show that such states do not really exist. When the Vedic texts appear to teach that they do exist, they are only affirming their existence in the sense that a man's existence is affirmed in the sentence 'That "man" you can see is only a post'. Still, the three states are real for us before enlightenment, and the Vedic and Smṛti texts give us useful information about them as viewed from that standpoint.

The main points of the Extracts of the present section, which deal with dream, are as follows. Viewed from the waking standpoint, dreams are seen not to have the degree of causal coherence characteristic of waking experience and so to be unreal. When the upanishadic texts[1] seem to accord reality to dream, they must be taken as speaking figuratively. It is held that dreams may in certain cases indicate future experiences in the waking world. They derive from the merit and demerit accruing from past actions. They are the creations of the individual (jīva), but are illumined by the universal light of Consciousness (prajñā). Dreams are the products of nescience, or they would never be unpleasant.

Dreams being unreal, the dream-agent is unreal and is not held responsible for his dream-crimes on returning to the waking world. In truth, the real element in the soul is not touched by waking experience either, and reflection on dream-experience is an aid to discovery of this fact. Dream-experience, viewed critically in the light of waking experience, is an aid to attaining the conviction that the light in all our experiences proceeds from the internal principle of Consciousness present within. It is clear, for instance, to waking reflection that the light and heat of the dream-sun proceed from the inner light of the dreamer, and this can help give us an insight into the fact that the light and heat of the sun in waking experience, too, depends on the inner light of our own Consciousness, a fact which could hardly become clear to us from an examination of our waking experience alone. Viewed from the standpoint of our waking experience, dreams appear to occur when the mind is withdrawn from the physical sense-organs at the external surface of the body and is inhabiting the subtle canals (nāḍī) that communicate between the physical sense-organs and the heart. So the Upanishads teach, but they are not dealing with ultimate truth here, but only with appearances as they strike an observer afflicted with nescience and in the waking state.

TEXTS ON DREAM

1. But if anyone thinks that because there is an exposition of the three states of waking, dream and dreamless sleep, (introduced between the two affirmations of the Absolute that come at the beginning and end of the passage),[2] it follows that the text means to teach the true nature of the transmigrant, he might as well turn his face towards the west when setting out to travel east. For the purpose of the texts in expounding the three states of waking, dream and dreamless sleep is not to declare that the Self is subject to these states of transmigratory experience, but to show, on the contrary, that it is entirely bereft of these states and is not subject to transmigratory experience in any form.[3]

❖

2. It is not correct to (quote Kaṭha Upanishad II.ii.8 and) say that the projections of the intermediate state (i.e. the dream-state) have absolute reality. The projections of the dream-state are a mere illusion (māyā), without a trace of reality. Why? Because, says the author of the Sūtras, 'Reality is but imperfectly manifest in dream'. That is, in dream the real does not manifest with the full characteristics of reality. What do we mean here by 'the full characteristics of reality'? Spatial, temporal and causal coherence and the absence of subsequent effacement which characterize the absolutely real are not achieved in dream. For example, there cannot be appropriate space in dream for a chariot. Large objects like chariots cannot find a place within the enclosed space of the body.[4]

Well, you might argue, be that as it may, the fact remains that one *does* see dreams outside one's body, because one sees objects belonging to other places. And the Veda, too, shows that dreams exist outside the body, as for example in the passage, 'The immortal one moves out from the body, and moves about wherever he wills',[5] where the distinction between the ideas of staying and moving out is only intelligible if the soul actually leaves the body.

But all this we deny. The sleeping soul cannot really go off to some place hundreds of miles away in a single instant and return as fast. And sometimes people will relate to us dreams in which the return is not included, saying, 'I was lying here in the land of the Kurus, overcome by sleep, was transported in dream to the land of the Pañcālas, and woke up again here in the land of the Kurus'. If he had really left the body he would have woken up in the land of the Pañcālas, and from the fact that he did not wake up there we conclude that he did not go there. And that body with which the dreaming person thinks that he has gone to another place is seen by the bystanders to remain at the place where he is sleeping. Nor do the distant places, as he sees them in dream, correspond exactly with their true nature. If he had really been on any travels he would have seen the places exactly as they are in the world of waking reality. And the Veda, also, shows that dreams take place within the body in the text, 'When the soul behaves thus in dream.... it is moving about in its own body'.[6]

Hence the other Vedic text, 'Moving out from the vile nest of the body'[7] must be explained as being figurative and meaning '*as if* moving out from the vile nest of the body'. For one who continues to dwell in the body but makes no use of it is 'as if' outside of it. This being so, the distinction between the ideas of staying and moving out[8] must be regarded as unfounded.

Time, too, is incoherent in dream. One may go to sleep at night and think that it is day in Bhārata Varṣa.[9] Similarly, in a dream lasting less than an hour one sometimes passes through many centuries.

Nor are proper causes found in dream for what we know or do. For one thing, the organs of sight and other senses have been withdrawn (from their seats in the exterior surface of the waking body), so that they are not really available to see the chariots and other objects that they appear to be perceiving. And how could the organs construct real chariots in an instant of time, as they appear to do in dream? And where would they get the timber for it? Moreover, these chariots and other creations of dream are effaced on awakening. They even undergo a kind of effacement in the course of the dream itself, since their end often contradicts their beginning. For sometimes in dream what is at one moment observed as a chariot suddenly becomes a man, and what is observed as a man suddenly turns into a tree. And the Veda denies the real existence of chariots or other objects in dream in clear words when it says, 'There are then no chariots or horses or roads'.[10] So a dream is a mere illusory appearance.

But if a dream is a mere illusory appearance, does it follow that dreams have no jot of truth whatever? 'No, it does not', we reply.[11] For a dream can indicate coming events, favourable and unfavourable. On this point there is the Vedic text, 'When a person who is in the course of performing self-interested sacrificial rituals sees a woman in his dreams, he should recognize the success of his ritualistic practices from that dream-vision'.[12] And there is another Vedic passage, '(Whenever someone dreaming) sees a black man with discoloured teeth who comes up and kills him...',[13] which teaches that dreams of this sort inform a person that he has not long to live. And the interpreters say that dreams of riding about on elephants indicate future wealth, whereas dreams of travelling about on a donkey indicate poverty. They also maintain that dreams concerning the texts to be recited, or about the presiding deity or about the materials used in the case of any impending sacrifice, may contain a particle of truth.

What the author of the Sūtras means here, however, is that although what is indicated by the dream may be true (in the context of the waking state), the sign that indicates it, such as the sight of a woman, etc., is itself a mere illusion as it is effaced on waking. So the doctrine that dreams are in themselves illusion still holds good.

This being so, when the author of the Sūtras says[14] 'There is a creation in dream, as the Veda says so', this has to be explained in a figurative sense. It is like when we say, 'It is the plough that keeps the oxen going'. Here it is not literally true that the plough carries the oxen along with it, but we may say it because the plough is the occasion for keeping the oxen going. Similarly we say figuratively that the sleeper creates chariots and the like and is the agent, when he is really only the occasion for them. In what sense is he the occasion? In the sense that he was the agent of certain good and bad deeds (in the past) which are the occasion for him to experience (now) joy or fear, and this in turn is the occasion for the appearance of the chariots and the rest in dream.

And there is another reason for citing the case of dream. In the waking state it is difficult to discern how the Self is of the nature of pure self-luminous light, as it is in direct contact with the senses and their objects, and is inextricably confused with external luminaries such as the sun. The case of dream is cited to enable us to discern the light of the Self as pure and self-luminous. In this connection, if the text under consideration were taken to be fundamentally concerned with the affirmation of the creation of chariots in the literal sense, then it could not at the same time be concerned with teaching that the Self was self-luminous. Hence the teaching (in other texts that have been cited) of the *absence* of any chariots, etc., in dream must be taken as fundamental, and the texts speaking of the *creation* of chariots, etc. must be taken as figurative....

So the real purpose of the present topic is to show that this creation that occurs in dream is not real like the creation of the world beginning with the ether and other great elements. Not that the latter creation is *absolutely* real. For it has been explained in commenting on the Sūtra 'Texts such as "A modification is a mere suggestion of speech" which show that the effect is non-different from the cause'[15] that the whole pluralistic world-appearance is a mere illusion. But before the practical realization of the fact that the Absolute is one's own Self has occurred, the world-appearance, beginning with the ether and the other great elements, has a lasting coherent structure, whereas the world-appearance set up in dreams is effaced for good daily. So it is significant if the author of the Sūtras here refers to dream as 'a mere illusion', as in the case of dream the word ('illusion') has a special (intensified) sense....

The soul (we have seen) is in its true nature non-different from the Lord. But its inherent knowledge and divine stature are concealed from it through its connection with the body. That is why the individual soul cannot create chariots and the like in dream *at will*. If it did have this power, no one would have an unpleasant dream, for no one creates unpleasant experiences for himself voluntarily.[16]

❖

3. Despite this (i.e. despite the fact that the Self is only identified with the intellect and other organs through false notions), the light of the Self (in its pure state) is inaccessible to any of the organs of knowledge in the waking state. And the light of the Self is then inextricably blended with the whole body of experience yielded by the intellect and the other internal and external organs, so that it is impossible to extract it from the midst of that experience as one extracts the stalk of a piece of muñja grass from its outer covering and holds it up to view. For this reason the text now goes on to exhibit it as it appears in the state of dream, in the words 'Being identified (with the intellect), it moves to and fro between the two worlds'....[17]

Wherever the Self is identified with an intellect, it seems to become whatever that intellect becomes. Therefore, when the intellect modifies itself into (the form of) the dream, the Self, too, attains the dream-state. And when the intellect throws off the state of dream, the Self does so too. Hence 'becoming identified with the dream' means illumining the dream-form of the intellect and also itself assuming that form (in appearance). In this form it rises above this world of waking experience, the world of the psycho-physical organism, the plane of secular and religious activity. That is, it stands illumining the dream-modifications of the intellect with its own distinct light. Hence it follows that the Self, in truth, must be of the very nature of self-luminous Consciousness, pure and void of agency and its factors and results. Meanwhile, because the Self remains indistinguishable from the intellect, the erroneous notion persists that it moves to and fro between the two worlds.[18]

❖

4. When the soul dreams, it goes beyond the forms of death.[19] Hence in dream the Self is itself the light.

Then the text proceeds, 'Others, however, say that a man's dream is only a phase of his waking experience'. The intermediate (sandhya) stage of dream, they imply, is not any special realm of its own, distinct from this world and from the next world alike, but rather belongs entirely to this world and is a phase of waking experience.

Well, what does it matter if it is? Listen to why it matters. If dream is but a phase of waking, then the Self cannot be distinct from the body and organs, but must be intermingled with them. And from this it would follow that the Self was not Consciousness by its very nature, and it is indeed just to refute the self-luminosity of the Self that other philosophers declare that dream is but a phase of waking. In this connection they advance a reason to show that dream is but a phase of waking and say, 'The individual only sees those things in dream — be they elephants or whatever — that he sees in waking'.[20]

But this idea is wrong. For in dream the sense-organs have ceased to function. One only sees dreams when the sense-organs have ceased from functioning. Therefore there cannot be any light in that state except the Self.[21] ...Therefore the Spirit (puruṣa) is self-luminous in dream.[22]

❖

5. But how does one know that one does not amass merit and demerit in dream, but merely experiences their effects? Should one not rather suppose that one acts in dream just as one does in waking, for the experience is the same in both cases?

To answer this question, the text says that whatever one experiences in dream is the result of (prior) merit and demerit and that one is not bound by it.[23] If a person actually did what he saw himself doing in dreams he would feel himself connected with it even after he had woken up. But people do not actually have this feeling. No one feels himself to be a criminal on account of crimes committed in dreams. Nor do people upbraid you or shun your company if they hear that you dreamed that you committed crimes.... The verse quoted in the text says '*As if* enjoying himself with women'.[24] Those who recount their dreams use the words 'as if' (iva), as, for instance, 'It seemed to me as if I was seeing a herd of elephants collecting together and making a stampede'. So there is no real agency in dream.[25]

❖

6. Is it not a fact, you will say, that in the state of dream, which is a state of vision, the Self has the same typical characteristics of transmigratory life that it has in the waking state,

even though it is dissociated from the body and organs? For example, it is at times happy and at times sad, and feels grief and attachment when separated from relatives. So should we not conclude that the soul has grief and attachment as its permanent (and hence real) characteristics, and that these feelings, and those of pleasure and pain, are not just attributed to it falsely through the error of imagining it to be connected with the body and organs?

But this is not correct, for the experiences of dream are illusory. When the Self, the subject of the passage, 'remains in the state of dream', then, as the text puts it, 'these are its worlds'. That is to say, these are the results of its past deeds. What are they? 'He becomes, then', says the text, 'an emperor, as it were'. His world is that of being an emperor *as it were*, not that he really is an emperor, as he would be if he remained an emperor even after he had returned to the waking state.

The soul attains, *as it were*, other states, higher or lower, such as that of a noble Brahmin. It 'ascends, *as it were*, or descends *as it were*' to the state of a deity or of an animal as the case might be. These states of being an emperor or the like are illusory, as is shown by the use of the words '*as it were*' (iva), and also because of the inconsistency of such experiences themselves. That is why one is in no way connected with grief and attachment or with any other emotions through separation from relatives in dream.

Perhaps you will say that just as the situations of the waking state persist consistently during that state, even so the situations experienced in the dream-state, such as those of being an emperor and the like, persist consistently as long as the dream lasts, and hence belong to the Self and are not falsely ascribed to it. But you must admit that we have already shown that the Self of the nature of Consciousness is different from the body and organs pertaining to the waking state, as also from the deities with whom it is identified (in meditation), and therefore that the notion of its identity with them is a false ascription arising through nescience, which does not represent a real fact. How, then, can this supposed identity, already killed and disposed of (in regard to the waking state), now rise up again, like a dead man wanting to return to the world of the living, and present itself as an example designed to show that dream-experiences are a genuine reality?

True, you will say, it has to be admitted that if the Self of the nature of Consciousness is distinct, then the notion of its identity with the body, organs and deities is a superimposition through nescience like the false vision of silver in nacre. But the separateness of the Self of the nature of Consciousness was not established in the course of showing its purity, but only in the course of proving that it existed as a distinct entity. The example of the identity of the Self of the nature of Consciousness with the body and organs can therefore be 'revived' — though it is admittedly in one sense non-existent (discredited) — because no argument can be considered to be merely repeated if any change is introduced into it.

But, we (Advaitins) reply, the fact remains that experiences in dream, like that of being an emperor, are not states of the Self. For what we see in dream is other than the Self, being a mere reflection (pratibimba) of the world of waking. Take the case of (one who really is) an emperor (from the waking standpoint) lying in bed and sleeping and dreaming, his senses withdrawn from activity, while his retinue are all asleep in different places (scattered all about the palace). In this state, let us imagine, he sees himself as another emperor, as it were, surrounded by his retinue just as he was when awake, and sees himself as if walking along with them in a procession and enjoying regal luxuries. Yet no other emperor in fact exists apart from the one lying in bed. There is no emperor actually found in the world who corresponds with that which the sleeping emperor sees in his dream, surrounded by his retinue and walking about with them by daylight. And it cannot be anything real that the emperor is perceiving in his dream, as no one whose senses are withdrawn from (outer) activity can perceive objects having colour and form. Moreover, it is only in one's body that dreams take place, and there cannot be any other body of the same kind as one's own body (hidden) inside one's own body.

One might object to this that a man lying in bed may see himself going about outside in the street. But the truth is that one does not see dreams outside one's own body, and with that idea in mind the text proceeds further. An emperor, it says, may take his retinue, and his officers and other servants, and may wander at will about the territory that he has conquered or inherited. In the same way, this Self of the nature of Consciousness wanders about the body at will in dream, though not outside it, withdrawing the sense-faculties from their seats (at the external surface of the body).... It means that, under the prompting force of merit and demerit and desire, it (the Self) experiences impressions (vāsanā) similar to things it has previously experienced. Therefore in dream it experiences 'worlds' (situations) which do not really exist and which are falsely superimposed on the Self as if they really belonged to it. And one should realize that this is exactly what happens in the waking state also. So it stands proved that the Self-consisting-of-Consciousness is pure and void of action, its factors and results. The 'worlds' (situations) experienced in waking and dream, consisting in things to be done and things to do them with, being of the nature of action, its factors and results, are objects for a subject. The subject, therefore, must be different from the objects he apprehends, the 'worlds' of dream and waking. He is the Self-consisting-of-Consciousness, free from all contamination coming from without.[26]

❖

7. But in what sense is it that he surveys the two worlds from the dream state? Where is he then based? How does he manage to do so? You want to know how all this takes place? Listen. The text says, 'According to his resources', where the reference is to his resources for travelling to another world, his basis or support for this. The soul, associated with whatever resources it has in the form of knowledge, action and previous experience[27] for attaining the goal of another world, stands on the threshold of departure, like a seed breaking into a sprout, and experiences both miseries and delights.... The soul beholds miseries and delights consisting in impressions from its experiences in previous lives. And it beholds (in dream) some fractional parts of the results of its (past) meritorious and vicious deeds which pertain to its next life, either through the force of its merit and demerit or through the grace of some deity.

But how can one know that one sees in dream the miseries and delights in store for one in the next world? We reply that this has to be accepted because in dreams we see much that cannot be substantiated from the present life. And it must also be remembered that a dream is never an absolutely novel vision. It is usually (in part) a memory of what has been experienced before. Hence the 'two worlds' (referred to in the text) are (the present world and the next world and) not (merely) the state of waking and dreaming.

Here the following argument might be raised in objection. The point has been made that when there are no external lights like the sun, the soul, associated with the complex of the body and its organs, enjoys experiences through the Self as Light, itself a distinct real principle. But no such distinct luminous principle, the objector might argue, really exists. For if we really knew of the absence of all suns and external lights we would be directly aware then and there of the self-luminous eternal Light *as a distinct principle*. But the fact is that the complex of the body and its organs is invariably perceived as permeated by the external lights. Therefore the Self as a distinct self-luminous principle is as good as non-existent, if not actually non-existent. If on the other hand, it were ever directly perceived as a distinct self-luminous principle void of all relation with matter and its effects, everything would be exactly as you claimed.

It is to answer this that the text proceeds, 'When he dreams'. When he goes into dream, then what does he take with him, and how does he attain that intermediary state (of dream)? The text speaks of 'this world'. It means the world of perceived waking experience. It is all-comprehending.... Of the 'all' in this sense he (the Self as dreamer) detaches a small fragment and takes it up — that is, he becomes affected by some impressions arising from the present life. Himself striking down his own body, he renders it unconscious. In the waking state the sun and the like (external luminous bodies) support the sense of sight, etc., so that there can be empirical experience through the body. The purpose of the soul's empirical experience in the body is that it should experience the fruits of its past meritorious and vicious deeds. And when its enjoyment of the fruit of its former meritorious and vicious deeds ceases in any given body, the soul is said to have struck down its own body, in that the above-mentioned cessation of enjoyment was due to the exhaustion of (a certain portion of) its own merit and demerit.

Then it constructs a dream-body for itself, like a magic body, out of the latent impressions left by its past experience. It is said to perform this construction by its own agency, too, because here the dreamer depends on his own personal merit and demerit. He then dreams dreams, which consist of his own light assuming the form of the perception of objects. His light illumines representations that consist in impressions through and through (i.e. without any objective counterpart). For here it is the mental mode, composed throughout of impressions, that shines as luminous. Here it is said to be self-luminous. With his own luminosity as object, and with his own Light as subject, separate by nature and unbroken, the Self enters the dream state, enjoying as object its own luminosity in the form of impressions. It is this process that is described by the words 'he dreams'. In this state and at this time, the Light of the Self is distinct and uncontaminated by intermixture with the external elements or with objects composed of them, either on the external or the mental plane.

Perhaps you will ask how, if what has happened is that a fragment of this world has been detached and taken up (in the dream-experience), we (Advaitins) can still claim in these circumstances that the soul is self-luminous.[28] But there is nothing wrong here, as whatever is taken up is an object for the soul's vision. It is the very presence of some form of an object in dream that makes it possible to show that the soul is then self-luminous, whereas it is not possible to do so when no object is present, as, for example, in the case of dreamless sleep. But when the light of the soul as associated with impressions is perceived as an object, then the unbroken self-luminous Light is perceived fulfilling its function of illumination without any intermixture from anything else, and radically separated from the organ of sight and from the whole body and its organs, like a sword drawn from its sheath. This shows that the soul is self-luminous in dream.

Now, you might ask how one could make a special distinction and say that the soul is (demonstrably) self-luminous here in dream. For in dream subject and object are both found, just as in waking. But we answer that in dream there is a difference. In the waking state the Light of the Self is actually *intermixed* with the activities of the senses, as well as with the mind in its higher and lower aspects and the external factors such as the light (proceeding from external luminous bodies). But in dream the senses are not in operation, and hence the external supporting factors such as the light (proceeding from external luminous bodies) are absent, too. The Light of the Self is separate from all and standing in isolation....

Well, but are not external objects apprehended in dream just as in waking? How, then, can you say that dream is different from waking because the senses are not then functioning? Listen. The text goes on to say that in dream there are no external objects like chariots. Nor are there any beasts to draw them, such as horses. Nor are there any roads on which to travel. The dreamer himself creates the chariots, the beasts and the roads.

But how can he create chariots and other useful objects when he has no trees for timber to make them from? We reply: Has it not already been said, 'Breaking off a fragment of this all-comprehending world, he strikes down the body and himself creates'? The fragment is the mental modification, consisting of an impression of past experience in this waking world. This is what he breaks off. And under the impulse of his merit and demerit, the impressions of chariots and other objects of past experience assume visible form as modifications of his mind. That is what was meant before when it was said, 'He creates'. And it is exactly the same thing that the text refers to now in saying 'He creates chariots and the like'. But in fact there are neither sense-organs, nor external luminaries like the sun to help the sense-organs, nor objects like chariots being revealed by them. There are only the impressions of all these arising from past experience of them (in the waking state). These impressions now lie in mental modifications arising under the impulse of past merit and demerit, which latter impulse is the sole cause of their being perceived at all. The light under which they are seen is the unbroken Light of the Self, separated and solitary like a sword drawn from its sheath.

There are then no delights (in the sense of delights arising from external objects), such as those proceeding from the birth of a son, etc., in all their varying degrees of intensity. There are no pools or tanks or rivers. He creates them himself in the form of impressions. Wherefore, 'He is himself the agent'. As we have explained, this means that his merit and demerit are the causes of the rise of mental modifications bearing these impressions. There is no question of action in the literal sense, as the requisite factors of action are not available, and there cannot be action without the requisite factors. In dream, there can be no hands or feet or other such instruments. But in the waking state, when all these are present, there the body and senses, lit by the (reflected) light of the soul, performed the work which is later (through its resultant merit and demerit) the cause of the rise of mental modifications bearing the impressions of chariots and the like in dream. It is in this sense (only) that the soul is said to be the 'agent' in dream.[29]

❖

8. The answer is now given to the question 'What is the luminous entity (deva) which sees dream?' And that answer is as follows. There is a certain intermediary period before the onset of dreamless sleep when the organs have already ceased to function and the Vital Energies, such as the outgoing breath and the rest, are awake and protecting the body. In this intermediary period, this luminous principle (the mind), having withdrawn into itself hearing and other organs, like the sun (withdrawing its rays at sundown), experiences wonders in dream. That is to say, it cognizes itself in different forms as subject and object.

Now, you will say, in the matter of experiencing wonders the mind can only be the instrument of some experiencer. How, then, can it be claimed that it enjoys experiences independently? Is it not the ultimate knowing principle housed in the body-mind organism (kṣetra-jña) that is the experiencer?

But there is nothing wrong with our position here. For the ultimate knowing principle enjoys independent activity only through the external adjunct of the mind. From the standpoint of the highest truth the ultimate knowing principle neither sleeps nor wakes, its appearance of waking and sleeping arises through the external adjunct of the mind alone....

Some, however, maintain that if the ultimate knower were associated with the adjunct of mind in dream, this would contradict its nature as self-luminous.[30] But this is wrong. Their error proceeds from an inadequate knowledge of the meaning of the Vedic texts. For up till liberation all empirical notions, including that of self-luminosity, themselves arise from the external adjunct, the mind, and pertain to the realm of nescience. We know this from such Vedic texts as, 'Where, indeed, there was another, as it were, there a seer who was one might see an object which was another'... and 'But when to the knower of the Absolute all this has become the Self, then what (else) should he see with what?'[31] Hence this objection is only made by those who have a very imperfect idea of the Absolute, not by those who are directly aware of the sole reality of the Self.

But (if self-luminosity were a mere conception of nescience) would not that undermine the text, 'Here (in the dream-state) this Spirit is self-luminous'? To this objection we reply as follows. You have said much less than you could have done. For (on your supposition that the Vedic texts teach about the states of dream and dreamless sleep as *facts*), the text 'It lies within the ether present within the heart'[32] would mean that (in sleep) the Self was confined to the inner portion of the heart, and then its self-luminosity would be contradicted even more obviously.

Very well, replies the objector, let us suppose that my view (that the Vedic text affirms the Self to be in a separate state in dream) has the defect (you suppose of contradicting its self-luminosity). But half the weight of your criticism is removed by the fact that the text implies that in dream the Self is *isolated* and self-luminous. But (the Advaitin maintains that) this is wrong. For the same Vedic text[33] later affirms that the Spirit lies in the subtle canals in (i.e. leading to and in) the pericardium. Hence on your theory it would then *actually* be connected with (and conditioned by) the pericardium and subtle canals (and hence its self-luminosity would still be contradicted). So your attempt to remove half the weight of my criticism by pointing to the Vedic affirmation of self-luminosity in dream was beside the point.

You will ask me (i.e. you will ask the Advaitin), therefore, how I myself explain the text 'Here (in dream) this Spirit is self-luminous'.[34] ....Lay aside your conceit and listen to the Vedic doctrine, for none of those who fancy themselves great scholars will be able to understand the Vedic doctrine in a hundred years if they retain their feelings of conceit. The self-luminosity of the Self is not contradicted when the soul is 'sleeping' in the ether of the heart or when it 'enters' the pericardium and the subtle canals. For the Self remains unconnected with them and can be shown to be quite distinct from them. Hence the soul can see impressions when, under the stress of the results of its earlier deeds, they become manifest in the mind through nescience as if they were a second object existing over against it, these impressions being awakened in the mind by the combined force of nescience, desire and past action. And the existence then of the Self as the self-luminous Witness, quite separate from the body and all its instruments of cognition, and from the impressions which it beholds as objects, could not be denied by even the most arrogant of logicians. Hence it was quite right to say that when the senses have been withdrawn into the mind, and the mind is not yet withdrawn into the Self (as it is in dreamless sleep), the latter, still associated with the mind, is able to see dreams.

To the question, 'How, exactly, does the Self "behold wonders"?' the text replies as follows. (The Self remains) associated with the impressions of the friend or son it has previously seen, and when these impressions are awakened it sees them, and then the notion arises, through nescience, that the impressions actually are the friend or son. Likewise, what has formerly been heard appears through impressions (in dream) to be heard again. Similarly, nescience prompts (in dream) the idea that one is repeatedly re-experiencing things that have been previously experienced in different places and in different quarters. This includes, according to the text, both what has been experienced in this birth and in former births, for there can be no impressions of what has not been experienced in any way whatever. And it includes also what has been heard about and thus only mentally experienced, both in this and previous births. It includes the real, such as real water, and also the unreal, such as water seen in a mirage. In short, itself all, the Self sees all, both what has here been enumerated above and what has not been enumerated, as it has all the impressions of the mind for its external adjunct. This is how the 'deity of the mind', assuming the form of all the various instruments of cognition, sees dreams.[35]

2. Dreamless Sleep

The close connection between dreamless sleep and liberation is one of the striking features of the teaching of the oldest Upanishads. It has been claimed that the connecting link here is the Vital Energy.[36] The Vital Energy was taken in the oldest Upanishads as the immortal element in man. It is the constant factor (the teaching ran) that 'remains awake' when the other factors of the personality are overpowered by dreamless sleep. All the other organs of man except the Vital Energy are periodically 'overcome by death' in the form of dreamless sleep.[37] But the Vital Energy is immortal. It does not 'die' either in dreamless sleep or with the death of the physical body. The Self is mortal in so far as it is identified with the mortal physical body and its organs in the waking state, but can be seen in its immortal form in dreamless sleep.[38] In dream, the full serenity of dreamless sleep is not attained, so it is called an intermediate state. In dreamless sleep the sense-faculties 'enter into' the Vital Energy, and they emerge from it again on waking.[39] In dreamless sleep, the physical body and organs seem actionless, but the Vital Energy continues tirelessly at work. Similarly, the conscious element in man remains conscious in dreamless sleep, even though there is nothing for it to know. When the Self emerges in its true state, the ego disappears. The realization of immortality involves the loss of the sense of individuality and of identification with a particular personality. It is not the doctrine of Christianity or of the theistic Vedanta of Rāmānuja and others, where the soul is held to be immortal as a particular individual. Yājñavalkya even says, 'There is no individual consciousness after death'.[40] When the Self emerges in its pristine purity it loses all limitations, including spatial limitations.[41] The 'Adhyātma Yoga' of the Kaṭha Upanishad rests on the teaching of the older Upanishads that dreamless sleep gives the key to the true nature of the Self in that it reveals it as free from ideas, desire and ego.[42]

The Extracts from Śaṅkara's writings on dreamless sleep that follow are divided into three Groups. Those in Group A follow the general line of the old upanishadic teaching, summarized in the previous paragraph. Those in Group B, however, emphasize that the dreamless sleep of the unenlightened or spiritually ignorant man is not enlightenment. A seed of nescience remains which prompts him to awaken as the same finite individual who formerly passed into sleep from the waking state, and to continue his painful experiences of waking and dream until all seeds of ignorance are destroyed through enlightenment. The references to dreamless sleep in section 3 below (on Turīya) as one of the states of Prājña should be considered in connection with those of Group B here, as they emphasize the 'nescience' aspect and 'seed' aspect of dreamless sleep.

The last Extract of Group B, from the Commentary to Gauḍapāda's Kārikās, contains a remarkable distinction between the mind of the ignorant man 'dissolved' in dreamless sleep but big with the seeds of future suffering, and the 'stilled' state of the mind of the enlightened man, which enjoys discrimination (viveka) and is void of the 'impurities' called subject and object set up by nescience. The reference to meditative concentration (samādhi) — a subject on which Śaṅkara is not very eloquent elsewhere in his Vedantic works — and to the idealistic doctrine that the object as well as the subject of experience is only a modification of the mind, take us back to the days of Gauḍapāda when the formulation of the Advaita philosophy was still holding much common ground with the Mahāyāna, for instance the view that liberation (called Nirvāṇa by the Buddhists) arose from the 'stilling' (nirodha) of the mind through yoga practice. The passage is written with such conviction that it seems to rest on, or at any rate to be confirmed by, the author's personal experience in the course of his spiritual life.

Group C is very short and mentions states allied to dreamless sleep but not identical with it, namely coma (mūrchā) and deep meditative concentration (samādhi). The short final passage on samādhi shows how, outside his Commentary on Gauḍapāda's Kārikās, Śaṅkara brackets it with dreamless sleep and coma as a mere temporary refuge from subject-object experience, not to be confused with enlightenment through spiritual knowledge. It is a mere temporary state, dependent on the action of an agent.[43]

The student who compares Śaṅkara's texts on dreamless sleep with those of some of the later writers of his school will find a certain shift of emphasis. As Advaita developed into a scholastic system and came under attack from other schools, its adherents felt themselves forced to give more and more evidence to prove the existence of 'nescience' as a cosmic force, and one of the key principles in their system. Gradually the view gained ground that our reflections in the waking state on the experience in dreamless sleep 'I slept happily, I knew nothing' were in some sense a proof that we had 'perceived' nescience in dreamless sleep and could be cited as added evidence that nescience 'existed' as the womb of waking and dream experience. Nescience was treated as a kind of substance undergoing modifications, and virtually identified with Prakṛti or Nature in the manner of the Mahābhārata and Purāṇas, whereas for Śaṅkara, Prakṛti itself was an illusion set up by nescience. The doctrine of nescience as a substance undergoing modifications was used to explain the happiness of dreamless sleep.

The latter could not be due to any modification (vṛtti) undergone by the mind, as all agreed that the mind was dissolved in dreamless sleep. But even if the mind was not in play, the happiness of dreamless sleep could be attributed to a modification undergone by nescience (ajñāna-vṛtti) and 'perceived' directly by the Witness.[44] Another distinction unknown to Śaṅkara was that between 'Māyā' and 'Avidyā', with Avidyā conceived as a small parcel of Māyā pertaining to an individual. It was later taught that the mind dissolved into this 'Avidyā' (identified with the 'causal body') in dreamless sleep.[45]

All this represents a considerable development beyond what is found in Śaṅkara's texts, and verbally stands in contradiction with some of them. Several times in the Extracts to follow in Group A Śaṅkara emphatically denies that the absence of subject-object experience in dreamless sleep is due to nescience, and traces it to the natural non-duality of the Self, which precludes subject-object experience. But Śaṅkara did also recognize the difficulties of the old upanishadic view that the soul enters the ether of the heart in dreamless sleep and dissolves in the Absolute without being aware of the fact. Why, for instance, is a spiritual path taught at all if one gains liberation merely by falling asleep?[46] And how does one and the same individual persist between bouts of total dissolution in the Absolute? Śaṅkara solved these problems, as the Extracts in Group B will show, by appeal to the conception of the persistence of a 'seed' of nescience. And the question of whether or not the views of dreamless sleep current among the later members of his school were legitimate extensions of his own view depends very much on the value assigned to the word 'seed'. According to a text that has already been quoted earlier,[47] the seed should not be taken as anything positive, certainly not as a substance, but merely as that failure to realize that one is the infinite Self which is the prior condition for all those false representations of the Self that constitute our empirical experience.

Another point to bear in mind in trying to understand Śaṅkara's statements about dreamless sleep is that if, in many of them, he speaks of an 'absence of nescience', this is partly for a mere terminological reason. He most frequently used the term nescience to mean what he himself, in common with most other professional philosophers of his day, called 'false knowledge' (mithyā-jñāna),[48] namely a superimposition or positive misconception. Positive misconception is absent in dreamless sleep, coma and deep meditative concentration alike, and all sense of pain and limitation with it. But until positive knowledge that one is the Self of all is gained through the Advaita spiritual discipline, the 'seed' of nescience in the form of 'not-being-awake-to-the-real' remains, and the whole complex of impressions (vāsanā) that will awaken and emerge as waking and dream experience under the force of merit and demerit, remain with it. Only when there is the great awakening through the upanishadic texts communicated by a competent Teacher will the seeds of future empirical experience be burnt.

TEXTS ON DREAMLESS SLEEP: GROUP A

1. When, however, there is more than one word in the same grammatical case, such words can be taken (not as mutually contradictory but) as complementary, as in such sentences as 'He is asleep in his bed at home'. In this way we may understand the texts when they say that in dreamless sleep the soul sleeps 'in the subtle bodily canals (nāḍī), in the pericardium, in the Absolute'. The Veda teaches, too, that in dreamless sleep both the subtle canals and the Vital Energy are involved, as they are mentioned together in the same phrase in the text 'He (the soul) is in them (the subtle canals) when he is asleep and sees no dream, and then he becomes one with the Vital Energy'.[49]

And we have already learned from our discussion in connection with the Sūtra, 'The Vital Energy is, as the Kauṣītaki Upanishad affirms, the Absolute, for so we have to understand it',[50] that the Vital Energy is (in this context) itself the Absolute. Even from the passages where the subtle canals of the body are mentioned as the only resting place of the soul in dreamless sleep, such as 'In dreamless sleep he rests in the subtle canals',[51] we understand that the soul (in fact) rests in the Absolute alone, and that the subtle canals are only the instrument for this, as there is nothing in the passage which inherently contradicts the doctrine taught elsewhere that in dreamless sleep the soul unites with the Absolute. Our interpretation does not contradict the locative case in the words '*in* the subtle canals', as one who passes into the Absolute through these canals is still in them when the process is complete. Anything that is carried down into the sea by the Ganges is still 'in the Ganges' when it has just reached the sea.

Furthermore, the text is concerned with the passage of the soul to the Absolute (in the state of dreamless sleep) through these subtle canals (in the body) that are connected with rays emanating from the sun.[52] The soul is spoken of as 'gliding along' these canals in order to eulogize them. For the text first says, 'In dreamless sleep he rests in the subtle canals', and then proceeds, 'No evil touches him', which constitutes an eulogy of the subtle canals. And the text mentions the reason why the soul is then untouched by evil, saying that he is united with effulgence (tejas).[53] It means that he is then enveloped in the effulgence of the subtle canals in the form of 'bile' (pitta) and thus sees no external objects. Or else the word effulgence may here refer to the Absolute itself, as the word 'effulgence' (tejas) is used elsewhere to stand for the Absolute, as for example in the text, 'The Absolute, verily, is pure effulgence'.[54] The meaning is that in that state the soul is certainly united with the Absolute through the instrumentality of the subtle canals and that no evil touches it. And the reason for the soul's not being affected by evil when it is united with the Absolute is learned from other passages, such as 'All evils end here, for this world of Brahman is a place where all evil stands destroyed'.[55] This being so, we have to understand from the present text[56] that in dreamless sleep the soul lies both in the subtle canals and also in the Absolute, which is mentioned elsewhere (in the Veda) as its resting place in dreamless sleep....

By 'pericardium' (purītat) is meant the housing of the heart. That which is lying in the ether of the heart within the external housing may also be said to be lying within the housing, just as one who lives within a (house in a) walled city may be said to be living 'within the walls of the city'. And we have learned from the discussions over the Sūtra 'The small place, because of what follows'[57] that the ether of the heart is the Absolute. And we also know that the soul lies both in the subtle canals and the pericardium, because they, too, are mentioned together in a single phrase in the text 'Moving along towards it through these subtle canals, he rests in the pericardium of the heart'.[58]

The fact that Being (sat) and 'The Conscious One (prājña)' are the Absolute is well known. Hence these texts refer in practice to three resting places for the soul in dreamless sleep, namely, the subtle canals, the pericardium, and the Absolute.

But the real resting place is the Absolute alone, for the subtle canals and the pericardium are but instruments.

Furthermore, the subtle canals and the pericardium are the resting places of the soul only in the capacity of external adjuncts, and even this only in the sense that its organs abide there.[59] For nothing can serve directly as a resting place for the individual soul in its true nature (as the Absolute), but only indirectly, as providing the resting place for its adjuncts. For in its true nature it is self-established by its own power, being nothing different from the Absolute. Even when the Absolute is spoken of as being its 'support' in dreamless sleep, it is not meant that the Absolute and the individual soul are separate beings, respectively support and supported, but rather that the two are in reality identical. For the Veda says, 'In dreamless sleep, my dear one, he becomes united with pure Being, he goes to his own Self (svapiti, he sleeps = svam apīto, he is dissolved in his own Self)'.[60] Here the word 'svam' means the Self, and the text implies that the one in dreamless sleep (supta) attains to his own true nature.

Of course, it is also true that the individual soul is never anything but united with the Absolute, as it can never lose its own true nature. But in waking and dream it appears to acquire a foreign nature on account of its external limiting adjuncts, and it is only relative to this appearance that it is said to 'attain' its true nature in dreamless sleep. So it would be quite wrong to conclude from these (texts) that the soul in dreamless sleep was only occasionally united with pure Being, and sometimes not.

And again, even on the basis of admitting alternative

resting places, the account of dreamless sleep will remain exactly the same, consisting as it does of the cessation of all particular cognition. Being united with pure Being in that state, it is but right that the soul should have no subject-object cognition (vijñāna), for, as the Veda puts it, 'With what should he then have knowledge of what?'[61] Whereas if the soul lay only in the subtle canals or pericardium, one could not see any reason why it should not enjoy particular cognition, for there it would be in the realm of differentiation, and there, as the Veda puts it, 'Where there was, as it were, another, there a subject, who was one, might see an object which was another'.[62]

You might say that, even for that which abides in the realm of difference, extreme distance and other empirical factors are what cause the absence of cognition.[63] True, we could admit this if once we could admit that the soul were limited in its true nature, and it would then be as when we say of Viṣṇumitra that he has gone abroad and cannot see his own house. But the soul admits of no limitation except that apparently imposed by external adjuncts. Even if we admit that it is extreme distance and other empirical factors that produce absence of knowledge in the soul when it is identified with its external adjuncts, this will in no way affect the truth of the position that we are at present defending. For it will still be right to say that in dreamless sleep, when the external adjuncts (the mind and the senses) have ceased to function, the soul is for that very reason united with pure Being alone, and it is for the same reason that it has no particular cognition.

Our doctrine on this point is not concerned with affirming that the subtle canals and the pericardium are really the resting places of the soul in dreamless sleep, along with the Absolute and on a level with it. For no advantage would result to us from any alleged knowledge that the subtle canals or the pericardium were the resting place of the soul during dreamless sleep.[64] No particular advantages are mentioned anywhere in the Veda as being specifically connected with this knowledge, and it is nowhere declared to be a subordinate element in any other body of teaching which is concerned with man's advantage. Our concern, therefore, in enunciating the present doctrine, is solely to teach that the Absolute is the unfailing resting place of the soul during dreamless sleep. And this knowledge has real benefit for man, for it shows him that his real Self is the Absolute and that it is (by nature) free from the empirical experience (and pain) that characterizes dream and waking....

And because the Self alone is the resting place of the soul during dreamless sleep, it is always and regularly 'from the Self' that it (returns when it) wakes up. This is what is taught in a section on dreamless sleep where a question is asked, 'From whence did it return?'[65] And at the time of answering it is replied, 'Just as minute sparks rise up from a fire, even so all these organs rise up from the Self' and so on. The same truth is taught in the text, 'Having come from pure Being, they are not aware that they have come from pure Being'.[66] Had there been any question of alternative resting places for the soul during dreamless sleep, apart from the Self, the Veda would have taught that it sometimes 'came from' the subtle canals, sometimes from the pericardium and sometimes from the Self.

But here we take up a new point for consideration. When

there is an awakening from this union, is it only the one who attained union (with the Self in dreamless sleep) who awakens, or is it that there are other possibilities? For instance, should the formula be, '*Either* He (the Lord) or another (the individual soul) awakens?' And one might at first suppose that there were alternative possibilities. For when a drop of water is poured into a large body of water, it then just becomes that body of water. It would be difficult to take it out again, saying 'This is that exact drop of water'. And in the same way, when one is in dreamless sleep, he is united with the Supreme. That is what 'attaining union in dreamless sleep' means. He cannot then again emerge as separate, so the formula we would expect would be, 'Either He Himself (īśvara) or another, the individual soul, awakens'.

Against this, the author of the Sūtras replies, 'It is the same individual who goes to his own true nature in dreamless sleep and emerges from it again. It is he only, and not another'. Why is this so? The author of the Sūtras replies, 'Because of (considerations arising from) ritual, because of memory, because of the Vedic texts affirming the point, and because of the injunctions'. And we shall now proceed to explain these reasons separately.

First of all, he who awakens from dreamless sleep must be the same as he who went into it, because we see (in the case of the long rituals that last several days) people carrying on with the same rite after awakening from sleep. For (in the case of the long rituals) a person will proceed on one day to attend to the remainder of a rite he had begun the day before. And it would make no sense that it should be another person who took up for completion a rite that had been half carried out by someone else. So we conclude that (where there is a single rite lasting more than one day) it is one and the same person who performs the rite on the earlier day and the later day.

And here is the next reason (derived from memory) why the one who awakens must be the same as the one who went into dreamless sleep. If it were another, the later memory on the part of one who wakes up, 'I saw that there yesterday', would be inexplicable. For one person cannot remember the experiences of another. Nor would one's memory of oneself as 'I am that same' be explicable if it was another who awoke from dreamless sleep.

And we conclude also from certain Vedic texts that the one who awakens must be the same as the one who went to sleep. '(When that same one has enjoyed himself in this dream state and roamed about and seen good and evil things,) he hastens back in each case to the place where he started from in order to become awake'.[67] 'All creatures go to this realm of Brahman every day, but are not aware of it'.[68] 'Whatever they are in this world, whether a tiger or a lion or a boar or a worm or a moth or a mosquito or a fly, that they again become'.[69] These and other Vedic passages about awakening from dreamless sleep would not be intelligible if he who awoke from it was different from the one who entered it.

And the same conclusion follows from (the presence in the Veda of) the injunctions to perform rituals and symbolic meditation. Otherwise these injunctions would be useless. For on the view that he who awakens from sleep is not the same as he who entered into it, it would follow that he who simply went into dreamless sleep would be liberated. And if that were the case, what, pray, would be the point in rituals or meditation, which bring their fruit only at a later time?

And there is more. On the view that the one who awoke was different from the one who went to sleep, the one who awoke would be a second soul, and if he were taken as already in the midst of experiences in another body, this would involve an irrational and inexplicable break in the experiences associated with that body. And if, to avoid this difficulty, you assume that the first soul awakens in the body formerly occupied by the second soul (to fill the gap), you gain little. For what do you gain by supposing that the one who goes to sleep in one body awakens in another, in comparison with the ordinary belief that the one who goes to sleep in a given body awakens in that same body?

Again, if you say that the sleeper awakens liberated, it would follow that liberation had (a beginning and therefore) an end. And the re-awakening of one (who was liberated and so) whose nescience had ceased would in any case be unintelligible. The same argument serves to refute the view that it is the Lord (īśvara) who awakens. For He is ever bereft of nescience.

Again, on the hypothesis that the one who awakens is different from the one who went to sleep, one can hardly escape the twin charges of attributing to one person the results of deeds he did not commit and of removing from another the possibility of experiencing the results of actions he *did* commit. So we conclude that he who awakens is the same as he who went to sleep, and is not another.

It was urged above that it would be impossible for the

individual soul to emerge as such from union with the Absolute in dreamless sleep, in just the same way as it is impossible to pick up a drop of water that has been poured into a larger body of water. But this we deny. It is quite right to say that the drop of water cannot be picked up, as there is nothing to distinguish it from the rest of the water into which it has fallen. But the case of the soul uniting with the Absolute in dreamless sleep is not parallel, as here there are factors able to produce a distinction, such as work (merit and demerit) and the merit arising from meditations practised in the context of the Vedic ritual. Moreover, the presence of distinctions is possible even in things which mere human insight cannot distinguish, as is instanced by the power of the swan to distinguish water from milk (even when they are intermixed).

Again, there is no separate being existing apart from the supreme Being and in principle capable of being distinguished from it, as the drop of water was at one stage distinct from the larger body of water into which it fell. It is pure Being itself which, viewed in relation to its external limiting adjuncts, is loosely spoken of as constituting the individual soul, as we have many times explained. It is in these circumstances that, as long as there is association with the bondage pertaining to a particular adjunct, the notion of one's constituting a particular individual soul remains. If, however, there were association with the bondage pertaining to a different external adjunct, there would be experience of oneself as a different soul. Therefore, (since one retains a sense of one's own identity as an individual), it must be that one and the same external adjunct (i.e. the subtle body) persists through (the cycle of repeated states of) dreamless sleep and waking, just as (one and the same plant persists through the repeated cycles of) seed and sprout.[70]

❖

2. Now, said Ajātaśatru, with a view to explaining his meaning, listen while I give the answer to the question I raised earlier. The question was, 'When this soul was asleep, this "soul-consisting-of-consciousness", where was it and from whence (at the time of waking) does it return?'

At that time (i.e. the time of dreamless sleep as viewed retrospectively from the waking standpoint), through its 'consciousness' (vijñāna), through a certain faculty residing in the inner organ and brought into being through the nature of the external adjunct (the psycho-physical organism) of the soul, it withdraws into itself the powers of speech and the various other faculties of action and cognition, and rests in the ether of the heart, the ether in its pure natural form, not that (ether regarded as one of the five elements constituting the world and) familiar in ordinary experience. It is the ether in the centre of the heart that is meant, and here the word 'ether' means the supreme Self, which is the soul in its true nature.

It is not just a matter of resting in the ether (as if it were one separate thing resting in another separate thing), for we learn from another text 'He is then united with pure Being, my dear one'.[71] The meaning is that the soul throws off its nature as a particular self, which is created by its connection with the external adjunct called the subtle body[72] and 'rests in' (i.e. exists as) its own true Self in perfect transcendence (kevala).

But how do we know that when it throws off its function

of superintending over the body and senses it then 'rests in' its own Self? From the familiar expression. To explain what that is, the text goes on to say that when the soul absorbs the consciousness of speech and the rest we then say, 'Svapiti' (he sleeps). That ('svapiti') is the familiar way of designating the soul in that state. And it is a way of speaking that reveals its true condition in that state. 'Svapiti' stands for 'Svam apīti', which means 'He dissolves in his own Self'.

And if, while accepting that popular nomenclature suggests that in dreamless sleep the soul has a form other than the empirical one, you ask for some more definite proof, the text proceeds, 'At the time of dreamless sleep the organ of smell is held in abeyance'. The word 'prāṇa' here stands for the organ of smell, as the context of this passage is dealing with organs. For it is only in connection with the organs and having them for its adjuncts that the soul has its empirical nature. But in the state of dreamless sleep the soul has absorbed all its organs and faculties such as the power of speech and the rest (i.e. of the organs of cognition and action). As the text puts it, 'Speech is absorbed, hearing is absorbed, mind is absorbed'. From this we conclude that when all organs are absorbed, the Self remains established in itself, free from all division into action, its factors and results.[73]

❖

3. When the individual conscious soul sleeps, then, even when it dreams, it is pure and free from the characteristics of the objective sphere. And when it gives up that activity of seeing called dream and falls into dreamless sleep it attains its own natural purity (samprasāda), like water attaining its

natural purity when withdrawn from all contamination by other things from without...

The sense, then, is that when there is no particular knowledge, the individual conscious soul is in dreamless sleep (supta). But what is the succession of events leading to dreamless sleep? The text goes on to explain.

The hitās, being the subtle canals (nāḍī) called by that name, are products of food and drink in the body. They run, seventy-two thousand in number, from the lump of flesh called the heart to the lotus-shaped outer covering of the heart (the pericardium), which they pervade. But the word 'pericardium' is here used figuratively to mean the whole body, so that the canals in fact pervade this latter, branching outwards towards the outer periphery like veins on an Aśvattha leaf.

The heart is the seat of the intellect (buddhi) or inner organ (antaḥkaraṇa), and the other external sense-organs are under the control of the intellect resident in the heart. Under the force of merit and demerit, the intellect in the waking state impels the sense of hearing and the rest along the subtle canals, which intersect the body like the strands of a fishing-net, till they reach their respective seats in the ear-drum and the like, where it superintends their functions. The individual conscious soul pervades the intellect, illumining it with his consciousness. And when the intellect contracts, the individual conscious soul contracts in conformity with the intellect. This is the 'dreamless sleep' of the individual soul, and the experiences at the time of its expansion in the waking state constitute its 'enjoyment'. For it conforms to the condition of its external adjuncts, such as the intellect, in the same way that the (reflection of the) moon conforms to the condition (calm or ruffled, etc.,) of the water in which it is reflected. Hence when the intellect returns from the waking state and travels along the canals to the pericardium, the Self travels (appears to travel) with it and rests in the pericardium. But the word 'pericardium' here refers to the body as a whole and it means that the Self rests pervading all the parts of the body without distinction, as fire pervades molten iron. Although it remains quite unchanged in its own true nature, it is said to 'lie in the pericardium', because it conforms (i.e. appears to conform) to the (changes in the) intellect, which themselves conform to merit and demerit. For there is no real relationship with the body in dreamless sleep, as the text will say later, 'He has then passed beyond all griefs of the heart'.[74]

The text now goes on to give an example to illustrate how this state is free from all worldly griefs. Conceive a youth or a new-born baby, or an emperor whose subjects are in perfect control and who is invariably able to fulfil his word, or a Brahmin whose learning and good conduct have reached the highest pitch of maturity, and suppose that they have attained such a flood of bliss as to obliterate all suggestion of pain, and are resting in that bliss. The natural joy of those beings, the youth and the others, would be taken in the world to be the highest there is. And if they were to come to feel pain it would be because they had departed from their natural state, so that the text was but right in taking their state as an image of perfect joy. For these are all examples which are perfectly familiar and intelligible. It has to be understood that the reference is to the natural state of these beings in general, not to their particular condition in dreamless sleep alone, since the happiness of dreamless sleep is what the example is supposed to illustrate, and if there were no difference between the illustration and the thing to be illustrated there could not be any illustration. Even so does this individual conscious soul rest in its own natural state as the Self at the time of dreamless sleep, devoid of all the qualities of the world of transmigration.[75]

❖

4. Now, you might claim (against the strict Non-Dualist) that something other than oneself was always perceived. But this view is wrong, as it is contradicted by dreamless sleep and deep meditative concentration (samādhi), where no 'other' is perceived. Nor can you retort that the apparent non-perception of another in dreamless sleep is due to the mind being engrossed in something different from oneself but changeless (on the analogy of the arrow-maker so engrossed in the arrow he is making that he is aware of nothing else). For non-perception in dreamless sleep is total. Nor can you say that because an 'other' is perceived in waking and dream it must be real, for these two states are set up by nescience. That 'perception-of-another' which characterizes waking and dream is the work of nescience, for it does not occur except in the presence of ignorance (of the infinitude of the Self).

Perhaps you will say that the non-perception characteristic of dreamless sleep is also the work of nescience. But this would be wrong, as it is the essential nature of the Self. The essence (tattva) of a substance is not subject to modification, as it depends on nothing external. Modification can never constitute the true essence of the real, as it depends on action from without. It is the accidental features associated with the real that depend on action from without, and these constitute its 'modifications'. As regards the Self, the perception enjoyed in waking and dream is but an accidental feature. The true nature (svarūpa) of a thing, not dependent on any external factor, is its essence (tattva). That element in anything which depends on a second thing (like, for instance, the heat derived from fire in a red-hot iron bar) is not the essence of that thing, as it will not be found in it in the absence of the second thing. Hence, because non-perception (of objects) is the natural state of the Self, no distinctions are found in dreamless sleep as they are in waking and dream.[76]

❖

5. Now, this state of being the Self of all, liberation, the result of knowledge, void of action, its factors and results, where nescience, desire and action find no place, is taught to exist on the basis of a piece of immediate evidence. The subject has already been introduced in the words, 'When he is in dreamless sleep he desires no desires and dreams no dreams'.[77] And this form of his was said to be the Self of all and his 'highest world'. It is beyond desire....

And it is free from sin. By the word 'sin' is meant merit and demerit.... The state is also fearless. Fear, indeed is an effect of nescience, for it has been said, 'He conceives objects of fear through nescience'.[78] In denying the effect of nescience here, the text denies (by implication) the presence of the cause of that effect also, namely nescience itself. The fearless state is that state free from nescience....

Now, if the Self undergoes no destruction in this state of

dreamless sleep and rests in its own true form, why is it that it has no knowledge of itself as 'I am' or of external objects, as it has in waking and dream? Listen to the reason why it has no knowledge in the state of dreamless sleep. The sole reason why it has no knowledge is that it is a perfect unity.

To explain this further he gives an example, for one can clarify what one wants to say through an example. When in the world a man in a state of desire is embraced by his well-loved wife who is in the same state, he has no knowledge of anything outside himself as 'This is something separate from me', nor does he have any introspective knowledge of the form 'Here am I, happy or unhappy'. When he is not being embraced by her he knows everything, both inner and outer, being separate from it, but at the time of the embrace he did not know it, being sunk in unity with all. The same is the case with the soul, the experiencer in the body. Being separated (through nescience) from its salt-lump-like unity with the elements, it enters here into the body and senses like the reflection of the moon or other object entering the water. And this same soul, embraced by its own Self in the form of Consciousness in its real natural state of transcendent Light, becomes a perfect unity, the Self of all, with no internal differentiation, and knows no other object outside itself, and no distinction within itself, such as 'This am I, happy or miserable (or whatever the case may be)'.

It was in this connection that you asked, 'Why does he know nothing in this state of dreamless sleep, if he is then in his natural state as the Light of Consciousness?' I have now stated the reason, which is that he is now a perfect unity, like that of a man and his wife in embrace. And this implies that variety is the cause of particular cognitions. And it has already been said that nescience is the cause of variety, inasmuch as it is what creates the notion of objects other than the Self. Hence, when the Self is separated from nescience it attains perfect unity with all. There being then no distinction of knower, knowledge and known, how could particular cognitions arise? Or how could there be such a thing as desire in the Self as Light, when it is established in its own natural state?

And this is his form of perfect unity with all; this form of the Self as self-luminous Consciousness in its natural state is a form where all his desires are realized. Only he whose objects of desire are separate from himself, and so other than himself, fails to realize them, as individuals like Devadatta and the rest do in the waking state. But this form of the Self is not separated from anything in that way, and hence in this form the Self has realized all its desires.

One might raise the question, 'Is it that in dreamless sleep he is 'not separate' from things that are really other? Or is it that 'other things' really are his own Self?' To this question the text replies, 'Nothing other than the Self exists'. Why? Because in this form 'All his desires are the Self'. In dream and waking, the objects of desire have the form of being apparently separated from the Self and existing elsewhere. But (in dreamless sleep) that which is the real Self of this separate form has realized all its desires, because in it there is no nescience to set up the notion of anything else as 'other'. Hence this form of the soul in dreamless sleep is desireless, as there are no objects of desire. Also, it is, as the text says, 'Void of grief'.[79]

❖

6. In fact, however, the example of the man and woman in close embrace has been brought up to... establish the self-luminosity of the Self in dreamless sleep. Self-luminosity is present in dreamless sleep. But one is not aware of it because all is then one. But it should not be taken that the self-luminous light of the Self is anything that comes to it adventitiously, like desire, action and the rest.

The text first indicates this indirectly, and then goes on with the subject in hand. And that subject is the condition of the Self that is directly experienced in dreamless sleep, where it is free from nescience, desire and action. To say that (in dreamless sleep) the Self is beyond all relations is only to state a simple fact. Here the Self is beyond desire, has no evils and has nothing to fear. In this state, says the text, 'A father is no father'. What makes a father a father in relation to his son is the act of engendering him, and at the time of dreamless sleep the 'father' is severed from all relation with that act. Hence a father is no father, because severed from the act that produced the father-son relation. And we conclude that, by implication, the 'son' cannot at that time be a son of his 'father'. For it was that act of engendering that caused the relation connecting both of them. Hence at the time of dreamless sleep the Self is in pure transcendence. And the text says, 'Free from evil'.

Similarly, a mother is no mother. The worlds that have been gained or have yet to be gained through ritualistic action are no worlds (for the sleeper) because he has no connection with any ritualistic act. The case is the same with the Vedas. They lay down the ends and means and the relations between the two for ritualistic practice, and their verse portions are part of the ritual, in so far as they lay down what must be recited.

But whether they have been recited or have yet to be recited, they are connected with the sleeper only through his ritualistic action, and because he has gone beyond all connection with that action at the time of dreamless sleep, the Vedas are (for him) 'no Vedas'.[80]

❖

7. The word 'svapnāntam' here means 'dreamless sleep' as being in the middle between 'dreams' (svapna), the latter being taken as the state of seeing (in either dream or waking). Or the etymology may be through 'svapna-satattvam', meaning 'sleep in its true nature', where the implied meaning would also be dreamless sleep, as is shown by the text 'Dreamless sleep means that he has gone to his own Self'.[81] The experts in Advaita hold that it is only in dreamless sleep that the individual goes to the Self. When the mirror is removed, the reflection of the man that it contained goes back into the man himself. And in the same way, when the mind and the other organs cease to function in dreamless sleep, the supreme deity that has entered into the mind as the individual soul in the form of a reflection of Consciousness with a view to unfolding name and form, returns to its own nature, abandoning its form as the soul, where it has the name 'mind'. So it is clear that the word 'svapnāntam' here means dreamless sleep.

Where, on the other hand, he goes to sleep and sees dreams, those dream-visions, being associated with pleasure and pain, are the result of merit and demerit. For it is accepted that it is merit and demerit that cause pleasure and pain. And it is only with the help of nescience and desire that merit and demerit can function as causes of pleasure and pain, and of seeing those dreams as their effects. Hence dream is necessarily accompanied by desire and merit and demerit, the causes of continued transmigratory experience. In dream, therefore, the soul does not 'go to the Self'. And this is supported by other Vedic texts such as '(In dreamless sleep) he is not accompanied by merit, he is not accompanied by demerit, for he has passed beyond all sorrows of the heart', 'This (dreamless sleep) is his state beyond desires' and 'This is his highest bliss'.[82]

With a view to show that it is in dreamless sleep alone that we find the Self in its form as a deity, liberated from its condition as individual soul, the argument proceeds: My dear one, have a clear idea of what I am saying as I speak to you. When do we have dreamless sleep? When the sleeping man is referred to by the word 'svapiti' (he sleeps). This is the common term in the world, and it has reference to the condition of the one asleep. When a man is referred to by the term 'svapiti' (he sleeps) then he is in unity with Being, designated by the word 'Sat', the deity who is the special topic of the present section of the Upanishad. That deity, having first 'entered' into the mind, that is, come into association with the mind and other organs, then abandons his form as the individual soul and returns to his own form as pure Being (sat), that is, Being in the highest sense of the term (paramārtha-satya). He thus dissolves back into his own Self (svapiti = svam apigati). That is why ordinary people in the world refer to the soul at that time by the word 'svapiti', he sleeps. The text means that our use of this word, which has etymological implications, is an indication that in dreamless sleep the soul attains to its true Self.

But how is it that ordinary people in the world know that there is union of the soul with its true Self in dreamless sleep? The reason given is that the cause of dreamless sleep is the weariness engendered in the waking state. In the waking state, the soul becomes weary through expenditure of effort in connection with the experiences of pleasure and pain that supervene through merit and demerit. Then the organs become weary of their various functions and withdraw from them.... The Vital Energy alone remains awake, unweary, in the vile nest of the body, and then (in dreamless sleep) the soul proceeds to its own Self, the deity called 'Being' (sat), to get rid of its weariness. The accepted view of the people in the world that this weariness cannot be made good from any other source except that of becoming established in one's own true Self is justified. For (the present Vedic text confirms that) 'He goes to his own Self'.[83]

❖

8. But when in dreamless sleep that nescience which sets up the appearance of beings other than the Self has ceased, there is no (apparent) entity separated from oneself as another. Then with what could one see, smell or understand what? The One is embraced by one's own Self as intelligence (prajñā), of the nature of self-luminous light. One is then all serene, with one's desires attained, transparent as water, and all one on account of the absence of any second. For, if a second thing is distinguished, it is distinguished through nescience, and as that has now ceased, what is left is all one.

It is the Seer, because of its seeing, being of the nature of self-luminous Light (which is not due to any act of seeing, or, indeed, action of any kind), and is without a break. It is without a second, so that there is no second thing for it to see. This is the immortal, fearless state. This is the world of Brahman, that is, the world that *is* Brahman (the Absolute). O King, (says Yājñavalkya), at this time, the supreme Reality, having thrown off all distinct external adjuncts, such as the body and senses, shorn of all relationships, rests in its own Light....

This is the highest state of the soul. All other states from that of the creator-god (Brahmā) down to the meanest clump of grass involve embodiment, are imagined through nescience and are secondary because they belong to the realm of nescience. But this state is far higher than the state of the gods and other exalted beings, won through the performance of ritual and through meditations on the symbolic significance of elements in the ritual. It is a state of identity with the Self of all, where one sees nothing else, hears nothing else, knows nothing else. This is the highest glory.... But it is not within the compass of achievement through action, as it is one's own natural state (and so eternal and not adventitious).... It is one's highest bliss when compared with whatever joys are promoted by the contact of the senses with their objects, because it is eternal. 'That which is infinite, that is joy', says another text.[84] Where one sees another, knows another, that is perishable, inferior joy. But this is the opposite of that, so this is one's highest bliss. On a fraction of this bliss, set up by nescience and lasting as long as the contact of the senses with particular objects, all other beings subsist. Who are those other beings? Those who have become separated from this bliss through nescience and have become falsely imagined as other than the Absolute. Being other than the Absolute, they subsist on a fraction of this bliss, maintained by the contact of their senses with objects.[85]

9. The question arises (with regard to dreamless sleep): 'Where, then, did this soul then lie, O Bālāki? Where was it? Whence did it return?'[86] Here the problem is: when a person is awakened from dreamless sleep, the soul beyond the body and organs is awakened, but is there also some further principle beyond the soul in play? And the answer runs: 'When he is asleep and sees no dreams, then he is one with the Vital Energy' and again later 'From this Self the Vital Energies proceed to their respective stations, from the Vital Energies proceed the presiding deities, and from these the worlds'.[87]

The upanishadic doctrine is that in dreamless sleep the individual soul unites (in pure identity) with the Absolute, and it is from the Absolute that the world, beginning with the Vital Energy, springs forth. The dreamless sleep of the individual soul, a state of untrammelled purity,[88] represents its true nature (svarūpa), void of all particular cognition set up by adjuncts. Its return from thence is a fall. And it is declared by the Veda in this passage that that state must be known to be none other than the supreme Self.[89]

TEXTS ON DREAMLESS SLEEP: GROUP B

10. You ask how it is that all beings should attain unity with pure Being (in dreamless sleep) without being aware of the fact? Listen, and I will explain the matter to you with the help of an example. In the world, my dear one, bees make honey by gathering juices from various different trees and mingling them together into one substance, honey. And when they have been mingled together as one substance, the various juices no

longer feel a sense of their own distinctness as 'I am the juice of this mango or that jack-fruit'. They do not feel their own distinctness, for instance, in the sort of way intelligent humans feel when gathered together in a group. For the latter have feelings like 'I am so-and-so, the son of so-and-so and the grandson of so-and-so', and are in this way conscious of their own distinctness and are not confused with one another. The idea is that the different kinds of juices collected from the different kinds of trees, when once they are mingled together as honey, cannot be separately detected as sweet, sour, bitter or acrid, as the case might be. In the same way, my dear one, all these creatures mingle every day with pure Being in dreamless sleep, as also at death and at the world-dissolution at the end of the world-period. And yet they have no knowledge 'We are united with pure Being'.

This being so, they unite with pure Being without knowing that their Self is of the nature of pure Being. And so, whatever species they may belong to according to their previous merit and demerit, whether they are a lion or a tiger or whatever, they are stamped with the latent tendencies of the action and experience typical of that species, and (in the waking state) they feel 'I am a tiger' or 'I am a lion' as the case may be. And after they have entered pure Being in dreamless sleep, they come back from it again in the same form as before, whether tiger, lion, wolf, boar, worm, moth, mosquito or gnat. After their return they become the same as they were before their entry into dreamless sleep, because the latent tendencies of a creature, that have been generated earlier, last for thousands of millions of world-periods. For there is that other Vedic text, 'Birth takes place according to previous experience'.[90]

These creatures return to the same form they were in when they entered pure Being. But there do also exist others, different from them, who are completely intent on pure Being, their own true Self, who enter pure Being, the Self, subtle in character, and do not return from it....

But take the case of one who goes to sleep in his own house, wakes up and goes to a different village. Such a person would know, 'I have gone here from my own home'. Why are not those creatures who return from pure Being aware, when they awaken, of the fact that they have returned (from their own home) in the same way? Listen to a further example which will explain this point. Rivers like the Ganges and others which flow in the east keep to the east, and those like the Indus which flow in the west keep to the west. The water of these rivers is initially sucked up by clouds from the sea, then it falls as rain and assumes the form of these rivers such as the Ganges, and then again reaches the sea, and indeed becomes the sea. When those rivers have mingled with the sea they do not then know 'I am the Ganges' and 'I am the Jumna'.

In the same way, my dear one, because they had no knowledge when they mingled with pure Being, all these creatures likewise, the tiger and so forth, have no knowledge of the fact when they have returned from pure Being. They are not aware, 'I have returned from pure Being'.[91]

❖

11. The objects of one's desires are present in the ether of the heart, but they are concealed by untruth. How does this disaster occur? Just as those who have no clue to the presence

of a treasure hidden under the ground pass right over it, but do not find it, although it was available for finding, so all those souls afflicted with nescience go daily to the ether of the heart, which the text calls 'the world of the Absolute', meaning the world (state of consciousness) that *is* the Absolute. Yet they do not 'find' the Absolute — that is, they do not feel 'Today I have attained to the world (consciousness) of the Absolute'. For they are drawn away from their own nature by the unreal as explained above, that is, by such deficiencies (doṣa) as nescience and the rest....

But (it may be asked) does not even the one not possessed of this knowledge attain to the Absolute residing in the heart at the time of dreamless sleep, as we have the text, 'He is then united with pure Being, my dear one'?[92] It is quite true, he does. But there is a difference between the way he does so and the way the enlightened one does. Every soul is the Absolute and nothing but the Absolute, whether he is aware of the fact or not. But the enlightened one who has been awakened by the text 'That thou art' is conscious that he is pure Being and feels 'Verily, I am pure Being and nothing but pure Being'. In the same way, both the enlightened and the unenlightened attain to union with pure Being in dreamless sleep, but it is only the one who is *conscious* of this that 'goes to heaven' (in the form of consciously attaining the Absolute daily in the form of dreamless sleep). The text calls the Absolute 'heaven' in order to indicate that apart from what happens in dreamless sleep, on the death of the body, too, the knowledge of the enlightened one will necessarily bear fruit (and he will be once and for all united with the Absolute).[93]

❖

12. The text now goes on to say, 'When the individual soul is asleep'. Next it specifies perfect purity, as there are two kinds of sleep, namely sleep with and without dreams. Perfect purity implies the withdrawal of the functioning of all the organs. Then the soul is perfectly pure, because there is no turbidity from contact with outside objects. Hence it does not then experience any dream-vision — no dream made up of the mental manifestation in the form of objects. The sleeping soul has then entered these subtle bodily canals (nāḍī), which are filled with the element of fire from the sun as already described.[94] And this implies that it has penetrated to the ether of the heart through the medium of the subtle bodily canals. Because dream-cognition cannot cease before the attainment of union with Being, the locative case in the phrase 'in the canals' has to be understood in an instrumental sense as 'through the canals'.

When it is thus united with pure Being, no evil touches it, neither merit nor demerit. For the soul then rests in its own true nature. Evil can affect it when it is associated with the body and senses, but not when it is united with pure Being, its own true essence. For it is not then an object. An object, indeed, can be the object of the action of something different from itself. But nothing can in any way or through any cause be different from what is united with pure Being.

When the soul proceeds from dreamless sleep to the states of dreaming and waking this involves a fall from its own true nature. And the reason for this fall is, as we have already explained in the course of the Sixth Chapter (of our Commentary on the Chāndogya Upanishad),[95] that the seeds of nescience, desire and action have not yet been burnt up by the fire of knowledge of the Absolute.

When the soul is thus in dreamless sleep, it is totally pervaded by the subtle particles of fire from the sun present in the subtle bodily canals. Hence its organs do not proceed outwards through the subtle canals leading to the eye and other physical organs to perceive external objects. The soul in this state rests in its own Self, as the functions of its organs have been suppressed. So it was not wrong to say that it saw no dreams.[96]

❖

13. Another objection that was raised was to say that once all the distinctions that go to make up the world-appearance have disappeared (at the time of the world-dissolution at the end of the world-period), there could be no determining cause that could promote the rise of the world-appearance through the manifestation of distinctions again. But this objection is also inapplicable, as we can support our contention with an example. In the cases of dreamless sleep and of deep meditative concentration (samādhi), as well as in (coma and) other such states, we find that, although the natural state (of the Self) where no distinctions of any kind obtain has been reached, still, because wrong knowledge has not been altogether eradicated,[97] when one awakens from dreamless sleep or from deep meditative concentration there are distinctions just as before.[98]

❖

14. One should know that 'waking' means what is perceived through the senses, that 'dream' means memories of sense-experience, and that dreamless sleep is the absence of waking and dream, and is the Self, the supreme state. When the

ignorance pertaining to dreamless sleep, which is the seed of waking and dream, is burnt up through knowledge of the Self, it becomes powerless to generate anything further, like a burnt seed.[99]

❖

15. It has been said that through the awakening to the sole reality of the transcendent Self the mind becomes checked and its motion stilled. It indulges in no ideation, and, because there are no external objects, it subsides like a fire subsiding in the absence of fuel. And it has been further explained how in this state, where the mind is no mind, there is no duality. The text goes on to speak about this further.

The yogin should form an accurate conception of the condition of the mind when its motions have been stilled, when it is without any ideation and is possessed of discrimination.

Perhaps you will say that its condition when its motions have been stilled is the same as its condition in dreamless sleep, where all ideation is also absent. Since there are no ideas in its suppressed condition either, what could be the difference between the two states? But we reply that this objection does not hold. For the condition of the mind in dreamless sleep is one thing and its condition when stilled is another. In dreamless sleep it is swallowed up in the darkness and the delusion of nescience. It is dissolved into seed-form, retaining the latent impressions of evil and activity. In its stilled state, on the other hand, the seeds of nescience, evil and activity have been burnt in the fire of the awakening to the sole reality of the Self. In this state it is independent and free from all the dust of the passions. So the two states, as the Teacher (Gauḍapāda) says, are 'not the same', and it was right that one has to form an accurate conception (of the state of the mind when its motions are stilled to see how it differs from dreamless sleep).

He then goes on to explain the reason for the difference of the two states. In dreamless sleep the mind is dissolved. And hence it attains then to a seed-form of darkness, without any manifest distinctions, but associated with all the seed-like impressions of future experiences consisting in nescience and the other passions. But when it is in its stilled state the mind enjoys discriminative knowledge, and it is not dissolved, and hence does not assume a seed-state of darkness. Hence it was eminently reasonable to maintain that there was a difference between the mind in dreamless sleep and the mind in the state of deep spiritual concentration (samādhi).

When the mind is void of the two impurities of subject and object set up by nescience it becomes the Absolute, transcendent and non-dual. That is the fearless state, because of the absence of duality, which is the cause of fear. The Absolute is at peace and fearless, and so the enlightened one has no grounds for fear.[100]

❖

TEXTS ON DREAMLESS SLEEP: GROUP C

16. The state of coma cannot be accounted a stage of waking experience. For a person in coma does not perceive objects through his senses. Can we say, then, that the one in coma is comparable to the arrow-maker?[101] The arrow-maker may be awake, but his mind is so taken up with the task of fashioning the arrow that he is not aware of any other object. One might perhaps claim that the one who was in a coma, though awake, was aware of no other objects simply because his mind was entirely taken up with the pain arising from the blows that rained down upon him through staves. But this would be wrong, as in the case of one who is in a coma there is no consciousness. The mind of the arrow-maker remains active all the time, and, when questioned afterwards, he replies, 'For such and such a time I was aware of nothing but the arrow'. The one in a coma, on the other hand, replies, when he has regained consciousness, 'For such and such a time I was thrown into blind darkness, I was not aware of anything at all'. And one who is awake holds his body upright, whereas the body of one who is in a coma slumps to the ground. Therefore he is neither awake nor dreaming, as he has no consciousness whatever.

One cannot, however, say that he is dead, as there is the heat of life in him. When any living creature falls into a coma, if people cannot decide whether he is alive or dead, they feel his heart to see whether it is warm, and next his nostrils to see whether there is still any breath of life. If they cannot find any evidence of the breath of life, or of heat, they conclude he is dead and carry him off to the forest to burn him on the pyre.

If, however, they find either the breath of life or heat they conclude he is not dead and treat him to try to bring him back to consciousness. And because he revives, it is clear he cannot have been dead, for no one returns from the realm of Yama.

Well, you will say, if he was non-conscious and yet not dead, he must have been in dreamless sleep. But this is wrong, as the characteristics of the two states are different. The one in coma sometimes passes a long time without breathing. His body trembles. His face becomes distorted. His eyes dilate. The one asleep, on the contrary, has a calm face, breathes regularly, has closed eyes and a body that does not tremble. Moreover, the one who is asleep awakens at a mere touch of the hand, whereas the one in a coma cannot be awoken by a blow with a mallet. And again, coma and sleep arise from different causes, coma from blows with staves and the like, sleep from fatigue. Coma and dreamless sleep, too, are ordinarily distinguished in common parlance.

We conclude, therefore, as the only remaining possibility, that coma is but a state of semi-union with the Absolute. It is union with the Absolute inasmuch as there is no subject-object consciousness: it is not complete union, inasmuch as there are characteristics which differentiate it from dreamless sleep.

We are not saying that in coma the Self is half in union with the Absolute (brahman). What we are saying is that when it is in a coma the soul stands half on the way to dreamless sleep and half on the way to death. We have shown how a coma is similar to dreamless sleep. And it is also the portal of death. When there is more experience arising from the effects of past deeds to be worked out in the present birth, the mind and speech of the one in a coma return. But when there is no such experience left, the breath of life and bodily heat leave him. Hence those who have realized the Absolute speak of this state as one of semi-union.

As for the criticism that no fifth state beyond those of waking, dream, dreamless sleep and 'the Fourth'[102] is admitted, it will not stand. Coma is not admitted to constitute a regular 'state' of consciousness, because it is rare and occasional. It is, however, perfectly well recognized in ordinary speech-usage and in the technical language of medicine. Nor does it constitute any 'fifth state' on our view, as we simply regard it as a half-way stage towards sleep.[103]

❖

17. But all (the Self's experience of plurality) is explicable as caused by erroneous notions, as in a dream. And the same sort of illusion is found in a hypnotist's magic display (māyā). Nor are the evils of agency and enjoyerhood experienced in dreamless sleep and states of deep meditative concentration (samādhi) and the like,[104] where the continuity of one's erroneous notion of identity with the body and its appurtenances is broken.[105]

3. Turīya

We have already seen how the doctrine that the soul undergoes the three successive states of waking, dream and dreamless sleep is only an example of the typical Vedantic method of false attribution and subsequent negation (adhyāropa-apavāda). Śaṅkara has said[106] 'The purpose of the texts in expounding the three states of waking, dream and dreamless sleep is.... to show, on the contrary, that it (the Absolute) is entirely bereft of these states'. It is only the ignorant soul, practising memory and reflection in the waking state, that supposes himself to be afflicted by these three separate states. Deeper reflection, however, shows that since they appear to follow one another and to be mutually exclusive, the Self, as that which persists through them as identical, must be different from them. This should become clear from the Extracts to follow quoted from Śaṅkara's Commentary on the Māṇḍūkya Upanishad and the Kārikās of Gauḍapāda. Before proceeding to these texts, however, it will be necessary to say a little about a few of the special technical terms employed in the Māṇḍūkya Commentary, which hardly occur in Śaṅkara's writings except in that work.[107]

The Māṇḍūkya Upanishad equates the Self (ātman) with the Absolute (brahman) and speaks of it as divided into four 'quarters' (pāda). Four quarters had already been attributed to the supreme Spirit in the Ṛg Veda X.xc.3, where it is said that only one quarter is needed to compose all mortal creatures, three quarters of Him remaining immortal beyond the roof of the sky. A closer parallel to the Māṇḍūkya conception is provided by Chāndogya Upanishad III.xviii.2, where the Absolute is divided into four quarters (catuṣpad) for purposes of symbolic meditation. Ostensibly the Māṇḍūkya text provides a theme for meditation on the three audible components of the holy syllable OM as identical with the experiencer and his world of waking, dream and dreamless sleep, while the root and essence of the three components of the syllable OM, as well as of the three states of waking, dream and dreamless sleep, is declared to lie in a transcendent realm called 'the Fourth', which is not separate from the rest, inasmuch as it is their own true Self, and which is communicable only through negations.

As will become clear from the Extracts quoted below, Śaṅkara interpreted the teachings of the Māṇḍūkya as developed by Gauḍapāda as a form of metaphysical idealism. There is one conscious principle called Prājña, and it is this which, through illusion, appears to undergo differentiation into a waking experiencer and a world of waking experience, into a dreamer and his dream-world and into an undifferentiated state from which the two other states emerge. As the experiencer and his world of waking experience, Prājña is known as Vaiśvānara, a term going back to Chāndogya Upanishad V.vi-xviii and meaning 'common to all men'. As the dreamer and his dream-world, Prājña is known as Taijasa, the luminous principle, a conception which goes back to Bṛhadāraṇyaka Upanishad IV.iii.9. In dreamless sleep, speaking from the standpoint of ignorant waking experience, the individual experiencer 'becomes' temporarily identical with the Absolute, with the Self as 'the Conscious One' (prājña-ātman),[108] but he is not himself conscious of the fact. If the student attains to 'the Fourth' (caturtha), then he becomes consciously aware of his identity with the Absolute. Gauḍapāda substitutes the term Viśva (the All) for the Vaiśvānara of the Upanishad, and uses the more archaic word 'turīya' for the 'caturtha' of the Upanishad to mean 'the Fourth'. Neither the term 'turīya' nor its variant 'turya' occurs in the Māṇḍūkya, though the term 'turīya' occurs at Bṛhadāraṇyaka V.xiv.5 and 6, in another passage concerned with meditation texts and ritual, where the Gāyatrī metre, which has three metrical feet or 'quarters' (pāda), is also said to have a fourth foot beyond the physical world.

Śaṅkara, for his part, introduces three technical terms, Virāṭ, Hiraṇyagarbha and Avyākṛta (the Unmanifest), all of which derive from the more ancient texts, and with all of which we are already familiar. They are not actually found in the Māṇḍūkya or Gauḍapāda's Kārikās, but their use seems justified by the language of the Māṇḍūkya. Māṇḍūkya 3 refers to the Self in the waking condition as Vaiśvānara, having seven bodies and nineteen mouths. Tracing the doctrine of the seven bodies of Vaiśvānara Ātman back to the cosmological teachings of Chāndogya Upanishad V.xviii.2, and finding in the 'nineteen mouths' a reference to the individual experiencer, Śaṅkara interprets the Māṇḍūkya teaching as implying a distinction between a microcosmic and a macrocosmic aspect of Vaiśvānara. As microcosm he is 'Piṇḍa', the physical organism of the individual: as macrocosm, he is Virāṭ, the world of waking experience. As Śaṅkara remarks in Extract 1, the way in which the distinction between the microcosm and the macrocosm is conceived implies the fundamental identity of the individual with the cosmos, and contradicts the pluralism of the Sāṅkhyas and the secular philosophers.

'Piṇḍa', then, or the physical body of the individual, has no independent existence apart from Virāṭ, the material universe of which it forms a part. But, apart from this 'gross' (i.e. perceptible) body, the individual also has a 'subtle' body, imperceptible through the senses, composed of the impressions of his past actions. These impressions remain mostly latent and unmanifest, but they condition the fate of the gross body, and emerge into direct manifestation in dreams. Consciousness enjoying this experience on the microcosmic plane is labelled 'Taijasa' by Gauḍapāda. But, as we have already seen, Śaṅkara took all the impressions of the past experiences of all living beings collectively as constituting the one deity Hiraṇyagarbha, the Cosmic Intellect.[109] Just as the individual as a physical being (Piṇḍa) is non-different from the totality of physical beings (called Virāṭ), so the individual as constituted of subtle impressions, some manifest, some unmanifest, that have been engendered by past thoughts and deeds, is non-different from the totality of such impressions belonging to all creatures, this totality being called Hiraṇyagarbha or Cosmic Intellect. In dreamless sleep, the individual finds identity with the universal Consciousness or Prājña. But he is unaware of this identity, and consequently springs forth again to undergo dualistic experience and pain, even as, on the macrocosmic plane, Hiraṇyagarbha springs forth from the Unmanifest (Avyākṛta), which is nothing but the Self unknown.[110]

Thus Śaṅkara identifies Piṇḍa with Virāṭ (but not *vice versa*), and Taijasa with Hiraṇyagarbha, in the sense of affirming that Piṇḍa and Taijasa have no existence independent of Virāṭ and Hiraṇya-garbha respectively. He equates Prājña, as viewed from the standpoint of the ignorant student reflecting retrospectively in the waking state on his experience in dreamless sleep, with the Self in its unmanifest form, spoken of, on the macrocosmic plane, both as 'the Unmanifest Principle' (the seed-principle from which manifestation springs) and also as the Cosmic Vital Energy (prāṇa). These points should become clear from a perusal of the Extracts presently to follow.

Of these six Extracts, the first two are taken from Śaṅkara's Commentary on the Māṇḍūkya Upanishad itself. The second Extract is of particular interest as it shows how here, as elsewhere, Śaṅkara's doctrine is essentially a 'Via Negativa'. 'The Fourth' can only be communicated to the student through first attributing to it the false but recognizable characteristic of having the three 'states' of waking, dream and dreamless sleep, and then negating that very teaching in a later passage. Śaṅkara would be entitled to claim that this was the method of the Māṇḍūkya itself, as is clear from Māṇḍūkya 7.

Extracts 3 and 4 are from Śaṅkara's Commentary on Gauḍapāda's Kārikās. They follow the familiar pattern of provisional affirmation followed by negation. Extract 3 connects dreamless sleep with the Cosmic Vital Energy (prāṇa) and speaks of the individual as resting there in 'seed form' in the dreamless sleep state; but Extract 4, if it does not actually retract the notion of seed, 'de-materializes' it and interprets it epistemologically as the state of 'not-being-awake-to-the-real', which may be metaphorically called the 'seed' of further positive misconception in subsequent waking and dream experience. The last two Extracts, Nos. 5 and 6, bring our exposition of the purely theoretical part of Śaṅkara's doctrine to a fitting conclusion in that he there describes the non-dual principle of Consciousness that remains over when all illusion, duality and pain have been cancelled through the Advaita discipline. This teaching is admittedly embedded in some instruction about preliminary meditation on the symbolic significance of the component sounds of OM which belongs strictly to Chapters XIV and XV in Volume VI to follow, but the culminating point to be stressed is the identity of OM, Turīya and the Absolute.

TEXTS ON TURĪYA

1. 'Whose sphere is waking' means that waking is Vaiśvānara's sphere. 'With externalized consciousness' means 'who has consciousness of objects as distinct from himself', that is, whose consciousness *appears* through nescience as if it had something external for its object.

The text then says, 'He has seven limbs'. This refers to the earlier text,[111] 'The head of this Vaiśvānara Ātman is the shining heaven, its eye is the source of all colour (the sun), its breath is the devious one (the wind), its trunk is the all-pervading-one (the ether), its bladder is water, its feet the earth'. And this (Chāndogya Upanishad) text completes the seven limbs (on which the worshipper of Vaiśvānara Ātman is expected to meditate) with the mouth, consisting of the Āhavanīya fire,[112] which is a necessary factor in imagining the Agnihotra.

In the same way, the statement 'He has nineteen mouths' means that he has nineteen 'mouths' as gateways for knowledge, in the form of the five sense-organs, the five organs of action, the five functions of the Vital Energy, the mind (manas), the intellect (buddhi), ego (ahaṅkāra) and the imagination (citta).

This Vaiśvānara, thus qualified, experiences gross (perceptible) objects made up of (the five elements beginning with) sound through these 'gates' as above described. He is called Vaiśvānara because he leads (nayana) all (viśva) men (nara) to various states in (accordance with their good or evil deeds). Or else he is 'Viśvānara' because he is all (viśva) men (nara). Viśvānara is Vaiśvānara. He is called the first quarter because he is non-different from the totality of physical bodies. This is called the *first* quarter because the other quarters can only be known after this has been known first.

Well, you will say, all the Māṇḍūkya text here actually mentions is that this Self is the Absolute, and is distinguishable into four quarters. So why speak of its having limbs, like the shining heaven for its head (which is not a statement of truth but a mere theme for fanciful meditation)? But such an objection would be wrong. For the text simply means that this whole area of plurality, taken together with the elemental forces on the divine plane (ādhidaivika) has four quarters through (i.e. as associated with) this Self. When the matter is thus understood, it will be seen that, when all plurality ceases, the non-dual truth becomes established.

One has to see the one Self in all beings and all beings in the one Self, as has been briefly summed up in such texts as 'He who sees all beings in the Self alone'.[113] Otherwise it might be conceived that the inmost Self was limited by the body, as the Sāṅkhyas and other philosophers hold.[114] There would then be no difference between our doctrine and that of these (pluralistic) schools, and this would contradict the specification made in the Upanishads about '(one) without a second'. And it is generally agreed that the whole tenor of the upanishadic teaching is to proclaim the sole existence of the one Self of all. So the Māṇḍūkya was but right to speak of the seven limbs of the Self, since its ultimate purpose was to teach that the individual physical organism (piṇḍa-ātman) on the microcosmic plane (ādhyātmika) was nothing over and above Virāṭ on the plane of the divine cosmic forces (ādhidaivika), which was why it spoke of the 'limbs' of the latter in the form of the shining heaven (as head) and the rest. Moreover, there is an indication (of the identity of the microcosm with the macrocosm when the Teacher Aśvapati[115] condemns lesser meditations) in the words 'Your heads would have fallen off (if you had not come to me)'.[116]

The affirmation (here made) of the identity (of piṇḍa-ātman) with Virāṭ is to serve as an indication of the identity (of Taijasa) with Hiraṇyagarbha and (of Prājña) with the Self in its unmanifest form (avyākṛta-ātman). And this has been declared in the Madhu Brāhmaṇa (Bṛhadāraṇyaka Upanishad II.v.1ff.) in the passage beginning 'This luminous (tejomaya = taijasa) immortal Spirit (puruṣa) in this earth (embodied especially in the sun), and this (luminous Spirit) present in the body (of the individual), are one and the same'. The fact that Consciousness in the state of dreamless sleep is identical with the Self in its unmanifest form is evident from the fact of there being no distinctions (in that state). And this it is which also shows how, when all duality has ceased, the non-dual (reality remains).

Dream is the sphere of 'Taijasa'. Waking consciousness

with its various instruments (such as body and senses), though in truth a mere vibration of mind, appears as if it had an external object.[117] It leaves behind an impression of like nature (i.e. of a cognition appearing to have an external object). That mind, endued with impressions of this kind like a tinted cloth, appears (in dream to be knowing external objects) as in waking, but without there being any external factors present, and prompted (solely) by nescience, desire and the force of previous deeds....

The mind (in the waking state) is internal relative to the senses. And consciousness (prajñā),[118] when it assumes the form of the latent impressions[119] of the mind in dream, is known as 'the one whose consciousness is internal'. He is known as 'Taijasa' (the Luminous One) because he is the knowing subject in a state of consciousness that is without external objects, and is mere consciousness through and through. Viśva (= Vaiśvānara) has an object and experiences consciousness (prajñā) in a gross form. Here, however, (in the dream state), consciousness as mere impression is the object of experience, hence the experience is said to be 'rarified' (pravivikta). The renewed reference (now in the context of Taijasa) in the Māṇḍūkya to the seven limbs and nineteen mouths has to be understood as referring to distinctions in internal consciousness that are parallel with those of externalized consciousness, which have already been mentioned before. This second quarter is called 'Taijasa'.

Sleep (conceived as ignorance in general and) defined as 'not-being-awake-to-reality', is present in the mental modifications of waking and dream. Hence, when the qualification 'Where he is asleep' is introduced (in the Upanishad text under comment), it is to specify the state of dreamless sleep. That is to say, granting that sleep in the form of 'not-being-awake-to-reality' is common to all three states (of waking, dream and dreamless sleep), then it (further) distinguishes dreamless sleep from the other two.

It refers to that place or time when the one asleep dreams no dream and desires no desire. For in dreamless sleep no dreaming of a dream in the form of wrong perception, and no desire of any kind, is found, whereas they are found in the states of waking and dream. This state of his is the state of dreamless sleep.

All duality results from the oscillation undergone by the mind. It is divided into the two states (of waking and dreaming). Without losing its nature (of being full of further potential distinctions) this duality appears to become an indiscriminate mass, and, with all its (potential) differentiations intact, becomes an undifferentiated unity, like the day swallowed up by the darkness of the night. In other words, the cognitions resulting from the oscillations of the mind in dream and waking appear to become a single solid mass. This state is called 'massed consciousness' (prajñāna-ghana), because it is of the nature of non-discrimination. To say that it is 'massed consciousness' means that it is like when at night-time all (the plurality of daylight) seems to become an indiscriminate mass (through non-discrimination) on account of the darkness of the night. By saying 'massed-consciousness only', the Upanishad means that there is then present nothing other than consciousness. In calling it 'ānanda-maya' the Upanishad does not mean that it is all bliss through and through, but only that it is predominantly blissful on account of all the absence of effort and pain associated with the oscillations of the mind into the form of subject and object. For there is no question of absolute bliss. It is as when, in the world, one who is in a state of relaxation is called 'happy' or 'an enjoyer of bliss'. And this (dreamless sleep) is a state of complete relaxation that is enjoyed by the Self (prājña), whence he is called 'the enjoyer of bliss'. As the Veda says, (speaking of dreamless sleep), 'This is his highest bliss'.[120]

He (Prājña) is called 'the mouth of conscious experience' because he is the gateway to dream and waking consciousness.... He is called 'Prājña' (the Conscious One) because he knows all objects, including the past and the future. Even though asleep, he is still called Prājña (the Conscious One) on account of (his having been present as the illumining consciousness in) his earlier conditions (in waking and dream). Or else the name Prājña may be applied to him in dreamless sleep because he is present (as massed consciousness) in his own special nature, whereas in the case of the other two states (waking and dream, although he is present as massed consciousness) there is differentiated knowledge present also. This Prājña is the third quarter.

This Prājña in his true nature is the Lord of all. He, and not, as the philosophers of other schools hold, a being of a different nature, is the Master of all differentiations and of all the cosmic powers.[121] As the Veda says, 'For the mind, my dear one, is tethered to the Vital Energy'.[122]

This very Prājña is called 'the Omniscient One' in as much as it is He who is the knower of all in all conditions where distinctions exist. Entering within all creatures, He is their Inner Ruler and Controller. He is also the womb of all in the sense that He gives birth to the whole world and all its distinctions in the manner described. Wherefore He is the source and goal of all creatures.[123]

❖

2. Now, having come step by step, the text has arrived at the fourth quarter and teaches it in the words 'without internal consciousness, etc.' 'The Fourth' is beyond any use of words. Hence since it cannot be designated by words, it is taught simply by the negation of all particular characteristics.

But will it not follow that it is a mere Void? No, for there cannot be a misconception without a positive ground. The rope-snake, the shell-silver, the man for whom a post is mistaken in the dark, the mirage and the like, cannot be imagined without their respective substrata, namely the rope, the shell, the post and the desert.

Perhaps you will say that, if 'The Fourth' is the support of all imaginary entities beginning with the Cosmic Vital Energy (prāṇa), then it must be subject to designation by words, as is a pot or the like when it functions as the support of water — so that it does not have to be conveyed by negation. But this is wrong. For the Cosmic Vital Energy and the rest are unreal (asat), being mere imaginations like the silver and the rest. No relation (e.g. of support) can be affirmed to subsist between the real and the unreal through any use of words, since no such relation can exist. Nor can any other means of knowledge apart from verbal revelation establish the existence of the Self, as perception, for instance, can establish the existence of a cow, since the Self has no external adjunct (whereby it could be identified). (Nor can the Absolute be the meaning of any term, since terms refer initially to universals),[124] and the Fourth is not associated with any universal, as cow and the rest (are associated with universals such as cowhood), for it is void alike of universal or particular characteristics, being one without a second. Nor can the Fourth be referred to through any verbal noun, like 'a cook', as it is changeless (and hence actionless). Nor can it be referred to by any adjective like 'blue' for it is without empirically knowable qualities. So it cannot be designated by any word.[125]

Well then, you will say, it must be just a piece of useless nonsense, like (the notion of) a hare's horn. But this is not so. For when the Fourth is known as one's own Self, then all longing (tṛṣṇā) for the not-self ceases, as desire for the silver ceases when the shell that has been mistaken for silver is known for what it really is. When the Fourth is known as one's own Self, there is no longer any scope for such defects as nescience or longing or the like. Nor is there any reason to declare that knowledge of the Fourth as one's own Self can never occur, for the texts of the Upanishads culminate in teaching that very knowledge. Witness, for instance, 'That thou art'... and 'All this is but the Self'.[126]

This Self, which has an absolutely real form and an unreal form, has been declared to have four quarters. Its unreal form is set up by nescience and consists in the three quarters (Prājña along with Vaiśvānara and Taijasa, already mentioned) which correspond to a seed along with its sprouts, although they are (mere imaginations) like the snake imagined in a rope. The text now goes on to affirm the existence of the absolutely real form of the Self, which is not a seed and which corresponds to the rope in the rope-snake illustration. And it does so by negating the afore-mentioned three states as mere imaginations, like the snake.

You will say: 'What is the need of denying internal consciousness and all other characteristics of the Fourth? For you have declared that the Self has four quarters. And merely by the act of explaining the first three quarters it is already established that the Fourth is different from them, and therefore does not have their qualities like internal consciousness and the rest'.

But to argue thus is not right. For it is only through the negation of the snake that the rope can be known for what it is. And the aim of the text is to bring out how the Fourth is none other than that very Self which (apparently) experiences the three states of waking, dream and dreamless sleep. It is like the text 'That thou art'.[127] For if the Fourth were anything radically different from that which (from the standpoint of ignorance) undergoes the three states of waking, dream and dreamless sleep, then it would be impossible to communicate knowledge of its existence to the hearer, and one would have to conclude that the Veda was useless (which is absurd), or find oneself landed in the doctrine of the Void.

The Self is and remains one and identical. But it is imagined as having the three successive forms of internal consciousness (dream), external consciousness (waking) and massed consciousness (dreamless sleep), even as a rope is falsely imagined (successively as snake, stick and stream of water). But when, with the rise of an authoritative cognition (pramāṇa) negating the notion that the Self undergoes any of these three states, one simultaneously achieves the cessation of the notion of plurality in the Self — which notion is the only source of woe — then 'The Fourth' is known once and for all, and no further proof or discipline is required.

The case is like that of the snake falsely imagined in a rope. As soon as the rope is distinguished from the snake, the result is that the snake ceases to exist in the rope any longer, and knowledge of the rope is achieved once and for all, and requires no further proof or activity.

Some,[128] it is true, hold that when (an object like) a pot is known, the means of knowledge (pramāṇa) not only acts to remove ignorance of the pot but also acts positively to illumine it as well. But their position is absurd, like that of one who held that cutting something involved further action on one of the thing's parts after the parts had already been severed from one another. The truth is that the means of knowledge is applied merely to remove ignorance, and its work is done when the unwanted ignorance is removed, just as the purpose of cutting is to sever the parts, and cutting is complete when the parts are severed. Once the offending ignorance of the pot has been removed by a suitable cognition, there is no later separate cognition of the pot,[129] and no further result that the existing cognition could achieve.

In a similar way, when the three states superimposed on the Self have been discriminated from it (and seen to have been false), only the Fourth remains, and there is no longer the *possibility* of the further activity of negation, the undesirable notions of waking, dream and dreamless sleep having already ceased. For the distinction between knower, knowledge and known ceases immediately with the cessation of the notion that one is in the three states. Thus the Teacher (Gauḍapāda) will say, 'When the Self is known, duality is no longer seen'.[130] Subject-object knowledge cannot remain an instant after the cessation of duality. For to suppose that it could would entail (a new suppression of duality and so lead to) infinite regress, which would mean that duality could never cease. Hence it stands proved that the cessation of the three states of waking, dream and dreamless sleep, that are superimposed on the Self and are the source of all evil, occurs simultaneously with the authoritative cognition which negates them.

When the text says, 'It is not internal consciousness', it negates Taijasa. When it says, 'It is not external consciousness', it negates Viśva. When it says, 'It is not both internal and external consciousness', it negates any indeterminate state between waking and dream. When it says, 'It is not a mass of consciousness', it negates the state of dreamless sleep, for this is a state of non-discrimination which is a seed (of further positive wrong conception). And when the text says, 'It is not conscious (na prajñam)' it negates all agency in any act of cognition of an object. And when it says, 'It is not non-conscious (na aprajñam)' it negates non-consciousness (acaitanyam).

Perhaps you will object that internal and external consciousness and the rest are directly apprehended as belonging to the Self, so that, unlike the illusory rope-snake, they cannot be negated by a mere denial. But we reply that, since the states of consciousness come and go and exclude one another mutually, while pure Consciousness persists through them unchanged, it follows that the successive states are mere illusions, just like the different successive illusions such as 'snake', 'stream of water' and the rest that arise (in relation to a rope which remains one and the same). On the other hand pure Consciousness is real because it persists unchanged through all vicissitudes. You cannot object that it is absent in dreamless sleep, for dreamless sleep is something we actually *experience*! The Veda confirms this in the text, 'There is no break in the knowing of the Knower'.[131]

This being so, pure Consciousness is not an *object* of perception. Not being an object of perception, it is (as the text goes on to point out) not within the sphere of practical dealings (avyavahārya). It is not accessible to the organs of action. The text says it has no defining characteristic (lakṣaṇa) or inferential sign (liṅga). So it is not accessible to inference. Hence it is unthinkable, and also not subject to (direct) communication through words. Yet it is (as the text puts it) 'That which is real, because it yields the consistent notion of one Self (eka-ātma-pratyaya-sāra)', that is, it has to be accepted (as real) because we have the constant and unfailing notion 'This Self is One' persisting through the successive mutually exclusive states of waking, dream and dreamless sleep. Or else the phrase 'eka-ātma-pratyaya-sāra' should be interpreted to mean that if one becomes awake to the Fourth, the proof (sāra = pramāṇa) is the constant notion of one Self. And this is confirmed by the Vedic text, 'One's only meditation should be on the Self'.[132]

The text has now negated the notion that the Self has three different natures as internal consciousness, etc., in the three different states of dream, waking and dreamless sleep. It next goes on to deny the existence of all facets of those states in the words, 'The destruction of all plurality'. What remains is therefore 'at rest', meaning not subject to change, likewise desirable (śiva), and non-dual, or bereft of all distinctions, which are fictitious. It is called 'The Fourth' (caturtha), which means the same as Turīya (not because it is a fourth entity distinct from the three others but) because it is free from the successive states of dream, waking and dreamless sleep. 'That is the Self', says the text, 'that one should strive to know'. This is said on the analogy of saying, 'You should know the rope as distinct from the imagined snake, fissure in the ground or stick, etc. for which it was mistaken (although the rope and the snake are not in fact two real distinct entities)'. The Self is that which is communicated by texts like 'That thou art'.... When the (present) text says that the Self 'has to be known', this is said relative to (the notion of knower, knowledge and known prevailing in) the state of ignorance before enlightenment. When the Self has been realized, no duality renains.[133]

❖

3. This next verse is given to show that the triad of Viśva, Taijasa and Prājña is appreciated in the waking state alone.[134]

Viśva is experienced as the one whose chief function is to perceive gross objects in the 'mouth' (gateway) of the right eye. Compare the Vedic text, 'This Being known as Indha is the Spirit (puruṣa) in the right eye'.[135] It is Vaiśvānara with the quality of incandescence, that is called 'Indha'. And the one who sees in the eye (in the individual body) is one with the Self of Virāṭ (vairājya ātman) in the sun.

Perhaps you will say that Hiraṇyagarbha is quite different from the 'Knower-of-the-body' (kṣetra-jña), the one who sees in the right eye, the controller of the eyes, the master of the (individual) body? But the objection is wrong, for there is no intrinsic difference. The Vedic texts speak of 'The one Divinity (deva) present hidden in all beings'[136] and the Smṛti says, 'Know Me as the Knower-of-the-body in all bodies, O Descendant of Bharata!' and 'Standing within creatures as if differentiated by them, although not really differentiated'.[137] Though He is present equally in all the organs, He is specifically spoken of as present in the right eye to indicate that He is Viśva (the All), because His powers of knowledge are especially evident there.

Present in the right eye, He sees a patch of colour. He may then close the eye and dwell on the colour within his mind as if in a dream, seeing that colour manifest in a (remembered) impression (vāsanā). And the same activity occurs in the case of a dream. So the luminous being (Taijasa) in the mind (spoken of in connection with dream) is none other than Viśva.

And then all memory may cease. The Conscious One (prājña) will then be all one, a mass of consciousness, withdrawn into the ether of the heart, there being then no mental activity. It is only perception and memory that imply oscillation of the mind, for when they are absent what is left is subsistence as the Cosmic Vital Energy, without any particularization. For on this subject we have the Vedic text, 'The Vital Energy absorbs all these faculties'.[138]

The luminous being (Taijasa) illumining dreams is one

with Hiraṇyagarbha, as it dwells in the mind. And here we have such texts as, 'The subtle body or the mind' and 'This Spirit is identified with mind'.[139]

But is it not a fact, you will say, that the Vital Energy is differentiated out in dreamless sleep? The sense-functions, which are made up of it, are present.[140] What, then, does it mean to speak of the Vital Energy as 'the Unmanifest' (as the Advaitin does in this context?)

There is, however, nothing wrong in our position here. For in the Unmanifest there are no distinctions of time and place (and the same is true of the one in dreamless sleep). When (in the waking state) one feels identified with the Vital Energy, the latter is no doubt manifest. But in dreamless sleep the Vital Energy is not manifest, as those in dreamless sleep do not identify themselves with anything finite, there being then only the Vital Energy in general, void of all particularization in the body.

At the time of the dissolution of the Vital Energy (prāṇa-laya) at death, the Vital Energy of those who formerly identified themselves with limitations (in the waking state) persists as unmanifest. And, in just the same way, when (dreamless sleep as) a state of non-particularization comes over one who (in the waking state) has been identifying himself with the Vital Energy, the Vital Energy persists as unmanifest and as a seed of future fructification. The Witness, also, is the same in both cases. It is the Witness of the unmanifest Vital Energy.[141] And this Witness is identical with the (apparently multiple) 'Witnesses' of those who identify themselves with the finite (in the waking state). So that the author of the Kārikās was but right to classify consciousness in dreamless sleep (prajñāna) as 'having become one' and as 'a single mass'.[142] Because in this realm, as we have explained, there are no distinctions of time and space.

But why is the Unmanifest Principle (avyākṛta) called 'the Vital Energy' (prāṇa)? Because of the Vedic text, 'The mind, my dear one, is tethered to the Vital Energy'.[143] Perhaps you will say that the words 'the Vital Energy' must here stand for the Absolute, as the words 'Being only, my dear one' show that this is the principal topic of the passage in question. But there is nothing wrong here. For 'Being' is taken here as associated with the seeds of action.[144] No doubt the meaning of the words 'the Vital Energy' in that passage is Being or the Absolute. But the Absolute as 'Being' can only be expressed by the words 'the Vital Energy' or 'Being' if it is regarded as associated with the seed of future births of the individual soul. Had the Absolute in seedless form (nirbīja-rūpa) been meant, some such (negative) formulae as 'Not thus, not thus'.... would have been used....

Indeed, if the word 'Being' in the Chāndogya Upanishad passage at present under consideration were understood to mean pure Being without seed, those dissolved in dreamless sleep or at the end of a world-period could not emerge again. Or, alternatively, those who had been liberated would be reborn, as there would be no difference between them and the ones in bondage in point of having no seeds of future rebirth (after death or for re-awakening after dreamless sleep). Moreover, such a doctrine would render the upanishadic teachings on spiritual knowledge pointless,[145] as there would be no seeds to be burnt up by knowledge.[146] Hence, throughout the whole range of the Veda, Being is only called 'the Vital Energy' or referred to as the cause of the world when it is assumed to be associated with seeds....

The author will go on to describe separately[147] that seedless state of the being called 'Prājña',[148] its supreme and ultimately real state, in which it has no connection with waking and other states of the body and is known as 'the Fourth' (turīya).

Finally, the author of the Kārikās was but right to say that the Self was experienced in three different ways *in the body*,[149] because even the seed-state is experienced there, as is evidenced by the consciousness (of one who has awoken from sleep) 'I knew nothing'.[150]

❖

4. What is produced is an effect or fruit. The cause is what produces it, namely the seed. Viśva and Taijasa, as comprising both non-perception of the real and wrong-perception of the real, partake of the limitations 'cause' and 'effect' both. But Prājña partakes only of the limitation 'seed'.[151] And it is a seed only in the sense of being the 'bare-not-being-awake-to-the-real', and this is what conditions (nimitta) it as Prājña. But neither of these two limitations, that is, cause-nature or effect-nature, as non-perception of the real or wrong-perception of the real respectively is conceivable in Turīya (the Fourth).

But in what sense is it that Prājña partakes of the limitation 'cause'? And in what sense is it that neither of the limitations 'non-perception of the real' nor wrong-perception of the real' is conceivable in Turīya?

Prājña has no knowledge, as have Viśva and Taijasa, of

any external thing different from itself, born of the seed of ignorance (avidyā).[152] Hence it is limited only by non-perception of the real, by darkness, the seed of wrong perception. On the other hand (as the Kārikā under comment says), 'Turīya ever sees all'. Because nothing else apart from Turīya exists, it follows that it is ever all and sees all, so that it carries no 'seed' in the form of non-perception of the real. It follows from this that there is no wrong-perception either, for wrong-perception proceeds (only) from non-perception. There cannot be such contradictory qualities as absence of illumination or false illumination in that sun which is ever of the very nature of illumination....

Or else we may say, following the Vedic text, 'There is no other Seer apart from it',[153] that the expression (in the present text) 'it ever sees all' means that it is Turīya alone which, resting in all creatures in waking and dream, is the light (ābhāsa) which sees all....

Not-being-awake-to-the-real is called 'sleep' because it is the seed 'sleep'. For 'sleep' (in this sense) alone is the seed of the production of particular cognitions. This is the seed 'sleep', and the one associated with it is Prājña. But sleep, which is non-perception of the reality, is not found in Turīya, because the latter is eternally the Seer in its very nature. And so there is no limitation (which you could label) 'cause' in Turīya — that is the meaning.

Dream is wrong-perception, like the wrong-perception involved in seeing a snake where there is in fact only a rope. Sleep has been said to be darkness, of the nature of non-perception of the real. Viśva and Taijasa are associated with (both) sleep and dream (in this sense of the words). Hence they are said to be limited as (both) 'cause' and 'effect'. On the other hand Prājña has been said to be associated with sleep alone, free from dream, and so to be limited only as 'cause'. But the wise, the knowers of the Absolute (brahman), do not see either of these (limitations) in Turīya, because they are contradictory to its nature, just as darkness would be contradictory to the nature of the sun. Hence Turīya is said not to be limited either as 'effect' or 'cause'.

When does a person become established in Turīya? The reply is as follows. Dream (in the metaphysical sense we are here dealing with) occurs in the case of one who wrongly perceives the real in dream and waking, like one who reads a snake into a rope. The sleep (in the metaphysical sense) of someone not aware of the real is common to the three states (of waking, dream and dreamless sleep). Because they are both characterized by both sleep and dream (in the metaphysical sense), Taijasa and Viśva belong together in the same category. In this category the illusion is called 'dream', because in it wrong-perception predominates and sleep is secondary. But in the third state, (dreamless sleep), the illusion is just sleep, of the nature of non-perception of the real.

When these two illusions, those of wrong-perception and non-perception — belonging to the effect-state (dream and waking) and the cause-state (dreamless sleep) respectively, and consisting in the limitations 'effect' and 'cause' — come to an end, a person reaches Turīya. He then sees neither of these limitations and becomes established in Turīya.

This individual soul subject to transmigration is the one who is (in the metaphysical sense) asleep and sees dreams in the two states of dream and waking. It is through the dream, of the nature of illusion (māyā), proceeding from beginningless time, and including the two characteristics of not-being-awake-to-the-real (as seed) and wrong-perception-of-the-real (as effect) that he has such dreams as 'So and so is my father, so and so is my son, this one is my grandson, this is my territory, these are my cattle, I am their owner, I rejoice, I suffer, this is to my disadvantage, this other to my advantage'.

But when he is roused by a supremely compassionate Teacher who is conversant with the real meaning of the Upanishads and hears the words 'Thou art not of that nature, characterized by cause and effect: thou art that (ultimate reality beyond cause and effect)', then he becomes awake to this (truth).

What form does this awakening assume? Here in this (non-dual reality) there are none of the 'Six changes of state beginning with birth',[154] either within or without. Hence it is (as the Kārikā says) 'unborn', that is, void of all external or internal changes of state. Because it is not affected by 'sleep' in the form of ignorance (avidyā) or darkness acting as seed, the cause of birth and other (changes of state), it is called (in the Kārikā) 'sleepless'. That Turīya is 'sleepless' and therefore 'dreamless' also.[155]

❖

5. The Self has already been described as the syllable OM and as having four quarters, the subject-matter here being that which is expressed by the syllable OM.[156] The same Self is

now treated 'as a syllable', the subject-matter now being predominantly the syllable that expresses the Self. What is that syllable? It is 'OM' says the Upanishad. The term 'adhi-mātram' (in the text of the Māṇḍūkya Upanishad) shows that the syllable is here to be analysed into its constituent parts (mātrā). The quarters of the Self are the parts of OM, the latter consisting in A, U and M.[157]

The text now proceeds to state the correspondences more specifically. The Self in the waking state, the Self as Vaiś-vānara, is the sound A, the first constituent part of OM.[158] The text states that the point of similarity between Vaiśvānara and the A of OM is their all-pervasiveness. All speech is pervaded by the sound A, as is confirmed by the Vedic text, 'All speech is A'.[159] And Vaiśvānara pervades the world, as is shown by the text, 'Of this Universal Self (vaiśvānara ātman) the head is the shining light (of the heavens)'.[160]

It has already been remarked that the name and the named are one.[161] As the syllable A forms the beginning, so does Vaiśvānara. It is on account of this point of similarity that Vaiśvānara is known to be the sound A.

Then the text proceeds to declare the results that accrue to a person who knows this. He attains all desires and becomes first among the great ones.

The dream-state of the Spirit, called Taijasa, is the second part of OM, or the sound U. What is the point of similarity that shows this? The sound U is as if superior to the sound A,[162] as Taijasa is superior to Viśva (= Vaiśvānara). And the sound U comes between A and M, as Taijasa comes between Viśva and Prājña. Taijasa 'comes between' Viśva and Prājña in the sense that it shares a common character with each.[163]

The fruit accruing to him who has this knowledge is next stated. Whoso knows this prolongs the line of knowledge. His enemies no longer feel any enmity against him any more than his friends do. No one in his family fails to acquire knowledge of the Absolute.[164]

The dreamless sleep of the Spirit, called Prājña, is the sound M, the third element in the syllable OM. What is the point of similarity which shows this? It is known through the measuring. Viśva and Taijasa are, so to speak, measured by Prājña when they enter and leave it, when they dissolve into it and spring forth from it, like barley being measured with a measuring ladle. And in a similar way, A and U dissolve into M at the end of the pronunciation, and later come out of it again (when OM is pronounced afresh).

Or the point of similarity may be dissolution. When the M of OM is pronounced, the A and U dissolve into it and become one with it. Similarly, Viśva and Taijasa dissolve into Prājña and become one with it at the time of dreamless sleep. So the identity between Prājña and the sound M follows from this additional point of similarity.

Next the text states the fruit of this knowledge. One who knows all this 'measures all this', that is, he has a correct knowledge of the whole universe. And he 'dissolves'. That is, he becomes identical with the cause of the universe. The subordinate fruits here mentioned are but eulogies of the main discipline.[165]

...The OM with no constituent parts is the Fourth. It is the pure Self, beyond word and meaning, beyond speech and mind. It represents the dissolution of the universe, the blissful non-dual principle. When meditated on by one who has this knowledge, OM with its three parts is the Self with its three 'quarters'. Whoso knows this enters his real Self through his own Self. Such an one sees the highest Self and knows the Absolute. In his case, the third 'quarter', the seed-state, has been burnt up.[166] He has entered the Self and is not reborn, for the Fourth bears no seeds of further empirical experience. For when the rope and the snake for which it was formerly mistaken in the dark have once been distinguished, the snake disappears into the rope, and, being a mere impression of the mind (buddhi-saṃskāra), never again emerges in the case of those possessed of discrimination.

Different, however, is the case with those of average or dull minds, whom we call 'aspirants' (sādhaka). They are walking on the right path. They have become renunciates. They know how the parts of OM correspond to the 'quarters' of the Self. It is right and proper that they should meditate on OM as a symbol of the Absolute for the sake of knowledge of the Absolute.[167] The Teacher (Gauḍapāda) will explain this later[168] when he says 'There are three kinds of qualified souls treading the path'.[169]

❖

6. That which exists with empirical reality (saṃvṛti-sat), and of which an idea is formed, constitutes the worldly duality of subject and object. It is the basis of all empirical dealings from the teachings of the Veda down. It is called 'worldly' because it is never found dissociated from the world. Here the

reference is to the world of waking experience, and this is what is meant by waking experience in the Upanishads.

There is another sphere consisting of that which does not even have empirical being as an object, but of which an idea is nevertheless formed. This is called 'private' because it occurs in the absence of the gross world of waking experience. Yet it is (here) said to constitute a 'world', as it is an experience common to all living beings. This is called dream.

But there is another phase of being, which is neither an object nor an idea, and which neither knows nor is known in the empirical sense. This is 'the beyond'.[170] A world is a sphere of subject-object experience. Where this is absent, but the seeds of all future activity are present, we have dreamless sleep.

That is called 'knowledge' whereby one comes to know the supreme reality directly, first as the realm of waking experience, then as the world of dream, and finally as 'the beyond'.[171] The 'realm of the knowable' of the verse means the same three objects of knowledge. For nothing apart from these three can be 'known', since everything ever thought of by the philosopher falls within them. But that which has finally to be known through spiritual intuition (vijñeya) is different. It is the final reality, called 'the Fourth' (turīya), the Self as metaphysical principle (tattva), non-dual, unborn. This doctrine of 'knowledge' in its three stages, and of spiritual intuition beyond them, is ever proclaimed, says the verse, by those who see reality, those who know the Absolute (brahma-vid).

To begin with, there is knowledge of the three kinds of

knowables one after the other. First comes the gross world. Afterwards, when this is absent, there comes the private world. Then, when this is absent, comes 'the beyond' (i.e. the experience of dreamless sleep). Then, when these three have been eliminated one after the other, one knows the ultimate reality, the Fourth, non-dual, unborn, beyond fear or danger. When this occurs, that man of great intellect, being now himself the Self, attains to omniscience here in this very world. As his mind now comprehends that which transcends all empirical knowledge, his knowledge never leaves him. When reality is once known, that knowledge never departs. He who knows the supreme reality does not first acquire knowledge and then find he has to revise it, in the manner of the secular philosophers.

Because the three 'worlds' have been taught as having to be known one after the other, the idea might arise that they were real. The Teacher (Gauḍapāda) now produces further argumentation to show that from the standpoint of the highest reality they do not exist. The three worlds of waking, dream and dreamless sleep have to be rejected as non-existent in the Self, as an imaginary snake has to be rejected in the rope in which it is imagined. What really has to be known is the supreme reality, beyond all the four modes of judgement.[172] The true discipline is to become a monk and give up the three desires for a son, wealth and a 'world' (after death), and then to cultivate the qualities of wisdom (pāṇḍitya), child-like simplicity (bālya) and sagehood (mauna).[173] And psychological defects like attachment, aversion, infatuation and the like have to be eliminated. The monk must know from the beginning of the path[174] what he has to reject, what he has to know, what he has to cultivate and what he has to eliminate, as these are the means to success.

Relative to the things that have to be rejected, cultivated or eliminated, the Absolute that has to be intuitively known stands as an exception, and, (unlike the others), is real from the standpoint of the highest truth. The rest are mere figments of nescience. The knowers of the Absolute do not accept that absolute reality attaches to the other three classes, namely what has to be rejected, cultivated or eliminated.

Seekers of the Absolute must recognize that all souls are subtle, pure and all-pervading like the ether, by their very nature. They are also beginningless and hence eternal. To obviate the idea that, because he has spoken of them in the plural, the souls must be many, the Teacher (Gauḍapāda) goes on to say that there is no atom of difference in them anywhere.

Souls are only knowable as objects from the empirical standpoint, not from the standpoint of the highest truth. As the sun is ever luminous by nature and is of the nature of eternal light, so also are the souls by nature luminous from the first. It is not necessary to establish their existence, as they are eternally self-established. In their own intrinsic nature, there is no room for doubt as to whether they exist or do not exist. As for the seeker of liberation who finds in this way that he has no need, either for his own benefit or for anyone else's, to ascertain whether he is of the nature of pure Consciousness, any more than the sun ever needs any other light either for itself or for anyone else — such an one has achieved the state of blessed abstraction (kṣānti) in which he feels no need of acquiring further knowledge or fulfilling further duties. Then he becomes fit for liberation.

There is no need for taking active steps to achieve peace (liberation) in the Self. All souls are eternally at rest, unborn, and completely withdrawn by nature, homogeneous and non-different from one another. That is, the Self, as a metaphysical principle, is unborn, homogeneous and pure, and hence there is no need to *produce* the state of blessed abstraction or liberation. Action can have no effect on that which is eternally of the same nature.

The Teacher (Gauḍapāda) then goes on to explain how in the whole world only those people who have attained the highest reality avoid misery. All the rest are miserable.

Those who hold fast to the reality of distinctions, those who conform to the standards of transmigratory life, dualists who declare that reality is multiple — wandering about on the path of duality, imagined by nescience, and remaining there permanently, they lack purity and are called miserable. And this characterization is but right.

Next the author goes on to explain how those who are not men of high soul (mahātman) or wise (paṇḍita), and who are outside the upanishadic tradition, of low standing and little learning, cannot plumb the depths of the highest principle of reality.

If there should be some few souls, whether they be men or women, who acquire a fixed conviction about the existence of the unborn, all-homogeneous principle of reality, they alone will be the people of true metaphysical knowledge. Their path and their metaphysical knowledge will be quite incomprehensible to other people of ordinary intellect. For there are such texts from the Smṛti as, 'Even the gods will be bemused if they try to follow the path of one who has become the Self of all living beings and who is intent on their welfare, without any aims for his own personal advantage. They will no more be able to track the path of enlightened men than to track the flight of birds in the sky'.[175]

The knowledge of unborn, unmoving souls is itself unborn and unmoving, like the brilliance and heat of the sun. Such unborn knowledge does not bear on any external object. Hence it is called 'relationless' (asaṅga) and 'space-like'.

If, on the other hand, anyone acquiesces, in accordance with the view of the secular philosophers, in the idea of the rise of any other reality within or without, even if it be minute in size, a man so lacking in discrimination will never attain the relationless state (of identity with the true Self). All the less could we speak of his ignorance being destroyed.

But if we say that their ignorance will not be destroyed, does that imply that we accept that souls are *really* ignorant? By no means, says the Teacher. Souls are not by nature in bondage to nescience, desire and the like. They are free by nature, enlightened and liberated from the first.

How, then, do we say of some of them that they *become* enlightened? The enlightened spiritual masters use such expressions just in the same way as we say, 'The sun is shining' (when it has come out from behind the clouds), when it is in fact always shining, or as we say, 'The mountains are standing', even though they are always motionless.[176]

NOTES TO CHAPTER IX

References to Extracts are in bold type

1 E.g. Bṛhad. IV.iii.9.

2 I.e. the passage Bṛhad. IV.iii.7 to IV.iv.22.

3 B.S.Bh. I.iii.42.

4 From the waking standpoint, the dream is taken as occurring within the subtle canals inside the dreamer's (waking) body.

5 Bṛhad. IV.iii.12.

6 Bṛhad. II.i.18.

7 Bṛhad. IV.iii.12.

8 Referred to by the opponent above.

9 Bhārata Varsha means the then-known land-mass south of the Himalayas. It was considered that at night-time, even when the sun was not illumining Bhārata Varsha, it might be illumining Ketumāla Varsha, an unknown 'continent' to the far north-west. See Vācaspati's *Bhāmatī*, *ad loc.*

10 Bṛhad. IV.iii.10.

11 In what follows, it must be remembered that the Sanskrit language does not always distinguish between reality and truth. If a dream 'conveys a truth' it in a certain sense 'has reality'.

12 Chānd. V.ii.8.

13 Aitareya Āraṇyaka, III.ii.iv.17, trans. Keith, 252.

14 B.S. III.ii.1.

15 B.S. II.i.14.

16 B.S.Bh. III.ii.3-4 and 6.

17 Bṛhad. IV.iii.7. On the two worlds, see Extract 7, present section.

18 Bṛhad. Bh. IV.iii.7.

19 The 'forms of death' are those mentioned at Bṛhad. I.iii.28, a text which takes the Vedic hymn, 'From the unreal lead me to the real, from darkness lead me to light, from death lead me to immortality' and equates 'the unreal' and 'darkness' with 'death'. The term for 'going beyond the forms of death' (atikrānto mṛtyo rūpāṇi) used by Śaṅkara occurs several times at that point in the Upanishad (Bṛhad. I.iii.13-16).

20 A quotation from the text under comment. The exponents of this view reappear at the beginning of Extract 5, present section.

21 The light cannot flow from the sun for instance, as the eye is not functioning to perceive it.

22 Bṛhad. Bh. IV.iii.14.

23 It does not create further merit and demerit entailing further experience in the world.

24 Bṛhad. IV.iii.13.

25 Bṛhad. Bh. IV.iii.15.

26 Bṛhad. Bh. II.i.18.

27 Knowledge and action here refer to the merit gained from meditation on aspects of the Vedic ritual (see Vol.VI, Chap. XIV, section 1, below) and from the performance of the ritual and various other pious acts. The phrase 'previous experience' refers to secular skills acquired in previous lives which unconsciously prompt us to certain apparently instinctive forms of action. They range from what causes the baby to search instinctively for his mother's milk to the refined conditioning that prompts a painter to choose his art and

excel at it. Cp. Bṛhad. Bh. IV.iv.2, trans. Mādhavānanda, 491f.

28 The objector thinks that the upanishadic text must mean that fragments of the external world are literally taken up by the dreamer, so that his dream-world is not lit by his own interior light but by the light of fragmentary experiences of the light of external luminous bodies like the sun.

29 Bṛhad. IV.iii.7. **The Extract is from Bṛhad. Bh. IV.iii.9-10.**

30 Because it would not then be self-luminous, but would require the adjunct of the mental impressions derived from worldly experience to become luminous.

31 Bṛhad. IV.iii.31 and II.iv.14.

32 Bṛhad. II.i.17.

33 Bṛhad. II.i.19.

34 Bṛhad. IV.iii.9.

35 Praśna Bh. IV.5.

36 Heimann, 130-146.

37 Bṛhad. I.v.21.

38 Chānd. VIII.vii.1-3.

39 Kauṣītaki II.13.

40 Bṛhad. II.iv.12.

41 Chānd. VII.xxv.1.

42 Kaṭha I.ii.12. Heimann *loc. cit.*

43 B.S.Bh. II.iii.39, Gambhīrānanda, 497.

44 Vidyāraṇya adopts this view, P.D. XI.65ff., but it goes back to earlier times.

45 Hiriyanna (*Outlines*, 348), claiming that in dreamless sleep 'individuality persists', gives a doctrine of this kind as the standard Advaita view. But Śaṅkara himself strives to maintain the old upanishadic teaching, 'In dreamless sleep, my dear one, he becomes one with pure Being', Chānd. VI.viii.1.

46 Cp. Sureśvara, N.Sid. (prose intro.) III.58.

47 G.K.Bh. I.11, see above, Vol.I , Chap.II, Note 36.

48 Examples from Vātsyāyana's Nyāya Sūtra Bhāṣya IV.ii. 35 and Śabara's P.M. Bh. I.i.2 are quoted at Darśanodaya, 121.

49 Kauṣītaki IV.19 and 20.

50 B.S. I.i.28.

51 Chānd.VIII.vi.3.

52 Chānd. Bh. VIII.vi.2-3. See Note 102 to Chap.VIII, above.

53 Cp. Chānd. VIII.vi.3.

54 Bṛhad. IV.iv.7.

55 Chānd. VIII.iv.1.

56 Chānd. VIII.vi.3, already quoted earlier.

57 B.S. I.iii.14.

58 Bṛhad. II.i.19.

59 The intellect abides in the heart, and the faculties of sense-experience are withdrawn by it into the heart in dreamless sleep, both intellect and sense-faculties passing over to the heart along the subtle canals, as the intellect has already passed out from the heart along those canals to the external seats of the sense-organs at the periphery of the body during sense-experience in the waking state.

60 Chānd. VI.viii.1.

61 Bṛhad. II.iv.14.

62 Bṛhad. IV.iii.31.

63 So that the absence of cognition in dreamless sleep would be caused by empirical factors such as the defect (doṣa) of the non-functioning or malfunctioning of the organs, etc., and not by the absence of all duality through perfect unification with the Self. Śaṅkara rejects the notion here, but at Extract 11 below we shall find him speaking of nescience and other doṣas afflicting the ignorant man in dreamless sleep, following the sense of the Chāndogya text on which he is there commenting.

64 Revealed texts are significant and authoritative only if they can be shown to be of benefit to man. If not intrinsically of benefit to man, they must be interpreted as mere auxiliaries to those that are. See Vol.V, Chap.XIII, section 2, Extract 6, below.

65 Bṛhad. II.i.16, and see II.i.18 for the reply.

66 Chānd. VI.x.2.

67 Bṛhad. IV.iii.16.

68 Chānd. VIII.iii.2.

69 Chānd. VI.iii.9.

70 B.S.Bh. III.ii.7-9.

71 Chānd. VI.viii.1.

72 For the subtle body, see Chap.VIII, section 2, Extract 12, above.

73 Bṛhad. Bh. II.i.17.

74 Bṛhad. IV.iii.22.

75 Bṛhad. Bh. II.i.19.

76 **Taitt. Bh. II.viii.5.**

77 Bṛhad. Bh. IV.iii.19.

78 Bṛhad. IV.iii.20.

79 **Bṛhad. Bh. IV.iii.21.**

80 **Bṛhad. Bh. IV.iii.22.**

81 Part of the text under comment, Chānd. VI.viii.1.

82 Bṛhad. IV.iii.22, IV.iii.21 and IV.iii.32.

83 **Chānd. Bh. VI.viii.1.**

84 Chānd. VII.xxiii.1.

85 **Bṛhad. Bh. IV.iii.32.**

86 Kauṣītaki IV.19.

87 Kauṣītaki IV.20.

88 Reading niḥsaṃrodhatā, not niḥsaṃbodhatā. Cp. B.S.Bh. IV.ii.9, svacchatvāc ca apratīghātopapattiḥ.

89 **B.S.Bh. I.iv.18.**

90 An untraced text.

91 **Chānd. Bh. VI.ix.1 to VI.x.2.**

92 Chānd. VI. viii.1.

93 **Chānd. Bh. VIII.iii.2-3.**

94 Chānd. VIII.vi.2.

95 See Extract 10, present section.

96 **Chānd. Bh. VIII.vi.3.**

97 It persists in seed form.

98 **B.S.Bh. II.i.9.**

99 **U.S. (verse) XVII.25 and 26.**

100 **G.K.Bh. III.34-35.**

101 Ṛṣi Bodhya tells Bhīṣma at M.Bh. XII.178.12 (G.P. Ed.) that an arrow-maker was one of his spiritual teachers, as he saw him so absorbed in his task that he did not notice the passing of the king.

102 For 'the Fourth', see the following section. It is not strictly a 'state' (avasthā).

103 **B.S.Bh. III.ii.10.**

104 Swoon or coma would be included here.

105 **Bh.G.Bh. XVIII.67 (intro.)** *ad fin.*

106 The present Chapter, section 1, Extract 1, above.

107 Bṛhad. Bh. IV.ii.4, however, refers very briefly to the transition of the enlightened man from Vaiśvānara to Taijasa to Prāṇa (= Prājña) to the supreme Self.

108 Bṛhad. IV.iii.21.

109 Cp. above, Vol.II, Chap.VI, section 4, Extract 8.

110 Cp. above, Vol.II, Chap.Vl, section 4, Extract 7, *ad fin.*

111 Cp. Chānd. V.xviii.2.

112 The second of the three fires used in the more solemn Vedic sacrifices and that into which the oblations were poured.

113 Īśa 6.

114 Though the soul was conceived as all-pervading in space by the Sāṅkhyas, its experience was conceived as limited to a particular body-mind complex, taken as real. Hence it was conceived as individual and in that sense limited.

115 Aśvapati Kaikeya, who was apparently the brother of the

ill-fated Kaikeyī who wrought such havoc at the court of Daśaratha. Her son Bharata is said to have been staying with the sage-king, his uncle, at the time of the banishment of Rāma. Cp. *The Rāmāyaṇa of Vālmīki*, II.i.2, trans. H.P. Shastri, Vol.I, 157. For the identifying reference to Aśvapati Kaikeya, cp. Chānd. V.xi.4.

116 Chānd. V.xii.2.

117 This epistemological idealism represents the standpoint expounded at Vol.II, Chap.VII, section 3, Extract 6, above.

118 The non-Sanskritist should note the diacritical marks. Prajñā means 'Consciousness'. Prājña means 'the Conscious One'.

119 Śaṅkara here uses the term 'vāsanā' for 'impression', apparently synonymously with his use of the term 'saṃskāra' a little earlier. Etymologically, the term 'vāsanā' derives from the metaphor of the clinging of odours to receptacles, as when a jar of honey might retain a faint perfume of honey even after being emptied and washed. The term 'saṃskāra' derives from the moulding, altering or finishing-work of the potter or other artisan. Cp. Sanskrit (saṃskṛta) language = the single polished or cultured language of the priests and courts as opposed to the various 'natural' (prākṛta) languages or dialects of the people. But Vyāsa in his Bhāṣya to Yoga Sūtra II.13 says that vāsanās are those saṃskāras which produce memory. Śaṅkara, too, at one place makes the vāsanā a sub-species of saṃskāra. At B.S.Bh. II.ii.30 (Gambhīrānanda, 425) he says that the character of an individual is unconsciously conditioned by the stock of his dispositions (saṃskāra) inherited from his deeds in previous births. Those only which actually manifest as ideas or behaviour are vāsanās.

120 Bṛhad. IV.iii.32.

121 Contrast the later view, Sadānanda, trans. Nikhilānanda

section 43, which makes Prājña 'devoid of the power of Lordship'. Identification of Prājña with Īśvara is regular in Śaṅkara, which agrees with the present Māṇḍūkya text on which he is commenting (verse 6). Abundant references are given by Deussen, *System*, footnote 82, who, like Col. Jacob in his Notes to his ed. of Sadānanda (para 7, 145f.), points out the contrast with Śaṅkara.

122 Chānd. VI.viii.2. Śaṅkara here equates Prājña with Prāṇa after Kauṣītaki III.3, 'That which is Prāṇa is Prājña and that which is Prājña is Prāṇa'.

123 Māṇḍ. Bh. 3-6.

124 Cp. below, Vol.VI, Chap.XV, section 3, Extract 3.

125 Cp. above, Vol.I , Chap.III, section 3, Extract 2.

126 Chānd. VI.viii.7 and VII.xxv.2.

127 Chānd. VI.viii.7, etc. Sac, M.R.V., 83, refers here appositely to U.S. (verse) XVIII.4, which reads: 'The function of teachings like "that thou art" as associated with reflection (yukti) thereon is merely to negate the not-self element (yuṣmad-dharma) from the Self, itself already existent and evident as "I" (aham iti). (The process is) like the negation of the idea of a snake (falsely imagined) in a rope'. Cp. also below, Vol.VI, Chap.XV, section 3.

128 Sac, M.R.V., 85, explains that the reference is to a doctrine (still championed by Śaṅkara's younger contemporary Maṇḍana, and later by Vācaspati), that sentences, being composite, could not directly yield knowledge of the Absolute, so that an authoritative knowledge of the Self could only arise from further meditation and other practices performed after hearing the sacred texts. The view of Śaṅkara and Sureśvara was that the function of the 'means of cognition' (pramāṇa — acts of perception, inference and hearing of authoritative statements, etc.) was merely to

remove ignorance in relation to the object.

129 Negation of error and cognition of substrate are one indivisible act, like the rising of one pan of a pair of scales and the falling of the other. See P.P., 167, trans. Venkataramiyah, 129.

130 G.K. I.18. Texts dealing with the state of enlightenment have been collected together in Vol.VI, Chap.XVI, below.

131 Bṛhad. IV.iii.30.

132 Bṛhad. I.iv.7.

133 Māṇḍ. Bh. 7.

134 They are located, according to the following paragraphs, in the right eye, the mind (heart), and in the ether embedded in the inner chamber of the heart.

135 Bṛhad. IV.ii.2.

136 Śvet. VI.11.

137 Bh.G. XIII.2 and 16.

138 Chānd. IV.iii.3.

139 Bṛhad. IV.iv.6 and Bṛhad. V.vi.1. Taijasa has the individual mind for adjunct, Hiraṇyagarbha the totality of all individual minds for adjunct. Therefore, if Taijasa is present in dream, so is Hiraṇyagarbha. The upanishadic quotations confirm the presence of a luminous principle in the mind.

140 In dreamless sleep the sense-functions are present in potential or seed form, though absorbed in the Vital Energy. Cp. Chānd. IV.iii.3. In the Unmanifest, of which the Advaitins are here speaking, nothing should be 'differentiated out' and nothing should be 'present'. That is the burden of the objection.

141 It has been said that there are no distinctions of time and space in the Unmanifest. All agree that there is non-

manifestation after death, followed by fructification of seeds as rebirth, continuity being assured by the presence of a single continuous Witness. If this can happen in the case of death, there are no *a priori* grounds for saying that a parallel development is impossible in the case of dreamless sleep.

142 In the opening Kārikā, G.K. I.1.

143 Chānd. VI.viii.2. When it comes to rest in dreamless sleep, it rests in the Vital Energy.

144 Chānd. VI.iii.2, 'That divinity (Being) thought, "Well, let Me enter into these three divinities by means of this living self and let me then develop names and forms".' The words imply that Being-as-associated-with-the-unmanifest-seed-of-name-and-form is under consideration in Chānd.VI, and not pure Being. Cp. Sac, M.R.V., 58.

145 And therefore would stand self-condemned as an explanation of them.

146 Liberation would accrue merely through falling into dreamless sleep. This is absurd because it would render the upanishadic teachings useless and the office of the commentator is to explain their correct use, cp. Sureśvara N.Sid. III.58 (prose intro.) and IV.40.

147 G.K. I.10.

148 Deussen gives about 30 references from the B.S.Bh. alone to show that Śaṅkara regularly identified Prājña with Īśvara, cp. reference at Note 121, above. See also the remarks of Sac, M.R.V., 59-61.

149 That is, in the body of waking experience. We have already seen (Extract 3, present section, opening sentence) how the very notion that there are three states of the soul at all is an illusion peculiar to the waking state.

150 G.K.Bh. I.2.

151 Prājña is the Absolute, associated with ignorance of the fact that it is the Absolute, and hence with the seed of future empirical experiences, which constitute the various wrong readings of the Absolute that continue to arise as long as its true nature is not known. And yet this 'ignorance' as to its own true nature on the part of the Absolute is not to be traced to any external source. It is associated with the absence of any differentiation in the Absolute into knower and known. See section 2, Extract 5, above.

152 Reading with the G.P. Ed. ātma-vilakṣaṇam avidyā-bīja-prasūtam.

153 Bṛhad. III.viii.11.

154 Birth, existence, growth, transformation, decline and destruction. Cp. Bh.G.Bh. II.20, trans. Shāstrī, 42, footnote.

155 G.K.Bh. I.11-16.

156 A passage on a similar topic has already appeared above, Vol.II, Chap.VI, section 2, Extract 16.

157 Vaiśvānara, Taijasa and Prājña must be taken as corresponding to A, U and M respectively.

158 The syllable OM is analysed by Indian grammarians into A + U + M, but the word is not normally spelt AUM in Sanskrit. The 'O', however, should be pronounced in the manner of the Scots saying 'home', not as heard in southern England. The orthography of modern printed texts of G.K. I.24, I.28 and I.29 implies a mere nasalization (like French 'en') at the end of OM, and not a full consonantal 'm'. It appears that the word has both forms.

159 Aitareya Āraṇyaka II.iii.6. All speech is a modification of the 'ah' sound made when preparing to gargle.

160 Chānd. V.xviii.2.

161 Cp. above Vol.II, Chap.VI, section 2, Extract 16.

162 It modifies it.

163 In common with Prājña, Taijasa has the quality of absence of apprehension of reality. In common with Viśva, it has the quality of positive wrong perception of reality. Sac, M.R.V., 122.

164 This is a paraphrase of Māṇḍ. 10, the text on which Śaṅkara is now commenting.

165 Sac makes the following observations (M.R.V., 124f.). Knowledge of the identity of Viśva, etc., with the sound A, etc., is in each case a mere subordinate discipline. Although 'fruits' are mentioned for those who gain these items of knowledge, the mention of such fruits does not convert the texts into a series of injunctions to meditate on the identity of Viśva with the sound A and so on. For symbolic meditations are not the subject of the section. The subject of the section is liberation, and the mention of subordinate fruits for subordinate items of knowledge is made merely to eulogize the main discipline. The chief discipline is the knowledge that the syllable OM and the Absolute or Self are identical, and that neither of them is either a verbal expression or anything that can be expressed verbally. This knowledge is the means to liberation. Naturally it only arises after the practical discipline, to be outlined in Vol.VI, Chap. XV, below, has been carried out.

166 And *a fortiori* the dream-state and the waking state, of which the state of dreamless sleep is the seed.

167 In other words, for *them* the Māṇḍ. text prescribes a meditation, and they may feel themselves to be agents performing this meditation for the sake of an end. In the case of the enlightened ones, the text merely stands as a negation of plurality, without standing as an injunction to any action at

all. What else could a text stating the final truth do?

168 G.K.Bh. III.16.

169 Śaṅkara's texts on OM are assembled at Vol.VI, Chap.XV, section 5, below. **Māṇḍ. Bh. 8-12 selected.**

170 Śaṅkara preserves the Buddhist term 'transcendent' (lokottara) used by Gauḍapāda, but he interprets it to mean dreamless sleep, reserving final transcendence for the principle called 'turīya'.

171 I.e. as 'massed consciousness' in dreamless sleep.

172 Is, is not, is and is not, neither is nor is not. See Vol.VI, Chap.XVI, section 5, Extract 13 below.

173 See Bṛhad. III.v.1 and also B.S.Bh. III.iv.47- 50.

174 'From the beginning of the path' seems a forced interpretation of Gauḍapāda's word 'agrayāṇataḥ'. It is more likely that Gauḍapāda meant that the ethical values must be learned from the Mahāyāna. On the meaning 'Mahāyāna' for 'agrayāṇa', see entry for 'agrayāṇa' in Edgerton, *Buddhist Hybrid Sanskrit Dictionary, sub verbo* (p.5). Examples are given at V.S. Bhattacharya, Ā.Ś.G., 199f. See also Mayeda, *Authenticity of the Gauḍapādīya Bhāṣya*, 90.

175 M.Bh. XII.239.23-24, G.P. Ed. Vol.III, 584.

176 **G.K.Bh. IV.87-98.**

LIST OF GENERAL ABBREVIATIONS

In principle, works are referred to under their authors' names throughout the Notes, and the abbreviations occasionally used to distinguish between an author's different works should not cause any difficulty. Except for the two entries R.T. and Sac, the following list comprises those abbreviations that are used independently of any author's name. The list excludes the names of Upanishads on which Śaṅkara wrote commentaries, which are listed under his name in the Bibliography and readily identifiable there.

A.B.O.R.I.	*Annals of the Bhandarkar Oriental Research Institute*, Poona
Ā.D.S.	*Āpastamba Dharma Sūtra*
Ā.Ś.G.	*Āgama Śāstra of Gauḍapāda*
Ā.S.S.	Ānanda Āśrama Sanskrit Series, Poona
Ā.Ś.S.	*Āpastambīyam Śrauta Sūtram*, Mysore University
A.V.	*Atharva Veda*
B.B.V.	*Bṛhadāraṇyakopaniṣad Bhāṣya Vārtika* (Sureśvara)
B.B.V.S.	*Bṛhadāraṇyakopaniṣad Bhāṣya Vārtika Sāra* (Vidyāraṇya)
Bh.	*Bhāṣya* (i.e. Commentary)
Bh.G.	*Bhagavad Gītā*
Bh.G.Bh.	*Bhagavad Gītā Bhāṣya* (Śaṅkara)
B.S.	*Brahma Sūtras*
B.S.Bh.	*Brahma Sūtra Bhāṣya* (Śaṅkara)
B.Sid.	*Brahma Siddhi* (Maṇḍana Miśra)
C.P.B.	*The Central Philosophy of Buddhism* (T.R.V. Murti)
G.I.P.	*Geschichte der indischen Philosophie* (Frauwallner)

G.K.	*Gauḍapāda Kārikās*, included in Gambhīrānanda, *Eight Upanishads*, Vol.II
G.K.Bh.	*Gauḍapāda Kārikā Bhāṣya*
G.O.S.	Gaekwad's Oriental Series, Baroda
G.P.	Gītā Press, Gorakhpur
I.H.Q.	*Indian Historical Quarterly*
I.I.J.	*Indo-Iranian Journal*
J.A.	*Journal Asiatique*
J.A.O.S.	*Journal of the American Oriental Society*
J.B.O.O.S.	*Journal of the Bihar and Orissa Oriental Society*
J.O.I.B.	*Journal of the Oriental Institute*, Baroda
J.O.R.M.	*Journal of Oriental Research*, Madras University
J.R.A.S.B.B.	*Journal of the Royal Asiatic Society of Great Britain and Ireland, Bombay Branch*
J.U.B.	*Jaiminīya Upanishad Brāhmaṇa*
M.Bh.	*Mahābhārata* G.P. Mūla-mātra Ed., 4 Vols.
M.K.	*Mādhyamika* (or *Mūlamādhyamika*) *Kārikās* of Nāgārjuna
M.R.V.	*Māṇḍūkya Rahasya Vivṛtiḥ* (Saccidānandendra Svāmin)
M.V.	*Method of the Vedanta* (Saccidānandendra Svāmin)
N.S.	Nirṇaya Sāgara Press
N.Sid.	Naiṣkarmya Siddhi (Sureśvara)
N.Sū.	*Nyāya Sūtras*
P.D.	*Pañcadaśī* (Vidyāraṇya)

P.E.W.	*Philosophy East and West*, Honolulu
P.M.	Pūrva Mīmāṃsā
P.P.	*Pañcapādikā* (Padmapāda)
R.T.	Rāma Tīrtha (17th century commentator)
R.V.	*Ṛg Veda*
Sac.	Saccidānandendra Svāmin (modern author d.1975)
Ś.B.	*Śatapatha Brāhmaṇa*
S.B.E.	Sacred Books of the East Series, Oxford University Press, Oxford (reprinted by Motilal Banarsidas, Delhi)
Ś.Ś.P.B.	*Śuddha-Śaṅkara-Prakriyā-Bhāskara* (Saccidānandendra Svāmin)
Ś.V.	*Mīmāṃsā Śloka Vārtika* (Kumārila Bhaṭṭa)
T.S.	*Taittirīya Saṃhitā*
T.B.V.	*Taittirīya Bhāṣya Vārtika* (Sureśvara)
U.S.	*Upadeśa Sāhasrī* (Śaṅkara)
V.P.	*Viṣṇu Purāṇa*
V.V.S.	*Viśuddha Vedānta Sāra* (Saccidānandendra Svāmin)
W.Z.K.S.O.	*Wiener Zeitschrift für die Kunde Süd- und Ostasiens*
Y.D.	*Yukti Dīpikā*
Y.S.	*Yoga Sūtras* (Patañjali)
Z.D.M.G.	*Zeitschrift der Deutschen Morgenländischen Gesellschaft*
Z.I.I.	*Zeitschrift für Indologie und Iranistik*
Z.M.R.	*Zeitschrift für Missionswissenschaft und Religionswissenschaft*, Münster/Westfalen

BIBLIOGRAPHY

I. Texts of Śaṅkara

Aitareya Upaniṣad Bhāṣya, G.P. Ed., n.d. See Venkataramiah, D.

Bhagavad Gītā Bhāṣya (Bh.G.Bh.), ed. D.V. Gokhale, Poona, 1931. See also Śāstrī, A. Mahādeva.

Brahma Sūtra Bhāṣya (B.S.Bh.), ed. with the *Ratna Prabhā Ṭīkā* of Govindānanda, the *Nyāya Nirṇaya Ṭīkā* of Ānandagiri and the *Bhāmatī* of Vācaspati, by Mahādeva Śāstrī Bākre, N.S. Press, Bombay, 1934. See also S.S. Sūryanārāyaṇa Śastrī.

Bṛhadāraṇyaka Upaniṣad Bhāṣya, ed. H.R. Bhāgavat, Ashtekar Company, Second Ed., Poona, 1928. Also consulted: Ā.S.S. Ed. of the same work, with the *Ṭīkā* of Ānandagiri.

Chāndogya Upaniṣad Bhāṣya, Ā.S.S. Ed., Poona, 1890. Also consulted: H.R. Bhāgavat's Ed., Ashtekar Co., Poona, 1927.

Īśa Upaniṣad. See Saccidānandendra, *Īśāvāsya*. Also consulted: G.P. Ed. of Śaṅkara's *Īśa Bhāṣya*.

Kāṭhaka (usually referred to as *Kaṭha*) *Upanishad*, ed. with Shri Shaṅkara's Commentary and Sanskrit Notes by Saccidānandendra Svāmin, Adhyātma Prakāśālaya, Holenarsipur, South India, 1962. Also consulted: G.P. Ed. of same work.

Kena Upanishad, with the *Pada* and *Vākya* Commentaries of Shri Shaṅkara, ed. with Sanskrit Notes by Saccidānandendra, Holenarsipur, 1959. Also consulted: G.P. Ed.

Māṇḍūkya Upaniṣad and Gauḍapāda Kārikā Bh.(G.K.Bh.), G.P.Ed., n.d.

Muṇḍaka Upanishad, ed. with Shri Shaṅkara's Commentary and Sanskrit Notes by Saccidānandendra, Holenarsipur, 1960. Also consulted: G.P. Ed.

Praśna Upaniṣad Bhāṣya, G.P.Ed., n.d.

Taittirīya Upaniṣad. See Sac, *Taittirīya Upanishad Shikshāvallī* and *Ānandavallī-Bhṛguvallī*, with Shaṅkara's Commentary and Editor's Notes and Commentary. Also consulted: G.P. Ed. of *Taittirīya Bhāṣya*.

Upadeśa Sāhasrī with gloss of Rāma Tīrtha, ed. D.V. Gokhale, Bombay, 1917. Also consulted: *Upadeśa Sāhasrī* with Hindi trans. of Munilāla, Banaras, 1954. See also Jagadānanda, Mayeda and Alston.

Vivaraṇa on the *Adhyātma Paṭala* of the *Āpastamba Dharma Sūtra* in H.R. Bhāgavat, *Minor Works of Śrī Śaṅkarācārya*, 2nd Ed., 1952 (422ff).

(Attributed) *Vivaraṇa* on *Yoga-Bhāṣya* of Vyāsa on Patañjali's *Yoga Sūtras*, Madras Government Oriental Series, 1952.

For TRANSLATIONS of Śaṅkara's work, see under: Alston, Deussen, Gambhīrānanda, Hacker, Jagadānanda, Jhā, Leggett, Mādhavānanda, Mayeda, Nikhilānanda, A. Mahādeva Śāstrī, Thibaut and Venkataramiah.

II. List of other authors and works quoted

('trans.' denotes English translation unless otherwise stated.)

ABHINAVAGUPTA, *Īśvara Pratyabhijñā Vimarśinī*, 2 vols, Bombay, 1919 and 1921.

AITAREYA ĀRAṆYAKA: see Keith, A.B.

AITAREYA BRĀHMAṆA: ed. Aufrecht, Bonn, 1879.

ALSTON, A.J. (trans.), *The Thousand Teachings of Śaṅkara* (*Upadeśa Sāhasrī*), Shanti Sadan, London, 1990.

—, *Realization of the Absolute* (*Naiṣkarmya Siddhi* of Sureśvara), Shanti Sadan, London, 2nd. Ed. 1971.

BIBLIOGRAPHY

ĀNANDABODHENDRA: see *Yoga Vāsiṣṭha*.

ĀNANDAGIRI: standard sub-commentaries (ṭīkā) on Śaṅkara's commentaries and Sureśvara's Vārttikas consulted in Ā.S.S. Ed.

ĀNANDAPŪRṆA, *Nyāya Kalpa Latikā*, ṭīkā on B.B.V., Tirupati, Vols.I and II, 1975.

ANANTAKṚṢṆA ŚĀSTRĪ (ed.), *Two Commentaries on the Brahma Siddhi*, Madras, 1963. (Being the *Bhāvaśuddhi* of Ānandapūrṇamuni and the *Abhiprāya Prakāśikā* of Citsukha).

ANNAMBHAṬṬA, *Tarka Saṅgraha*, ed. and trans. Athalye, 2nd ed., Bombay, 1930.

ĀPA DEVA, *Mīmāṃsā Nyāya Prakāśa*, ed. (with comm.) V. Abhyankar, Poona, 1937. Ed. and trans. F. Edgerton, New Haven (Yale), 1929.

ĀPASTAMBA DHARMA SŪTRA: See Cinnaswāmī Śāstrī, Bühler, and Bhāgavat, *Minor Works*.

ĀRYA DEVA, *The Catuḥśataka*, ed. V. Bhattacharya, Calcutta, 1931.

ASHTEKAR: see Bhāgavat, H.R.

ĀTMĀNANDA, Swāmī, *Śaṅkara's Teachings in his own Words*, Bombay, 2nd. Ed., 1960.

AUGUSTINE, St., *Confessions*, trans. Sir Tobie Matthew, Loeb Ed., London, 1923.

— , *De Trinitate*, text and French trans. Mellet, Desclée de Brouwer, 2 vols, 1955.

BELVALKAR, S.K., *Lectures on Vedānta Philosophy*, Part I, Poona, 1929.

— , *The Brahma Sūtras of Bādarāyaṇa*, Poona, 2 vols, 1923 and 1924.

BERGAIGNE, A., *La Religion Védique* (3 volumes), Paris, 1883.

BHĀGAVAT, H.R., *Upaniṣadbhāṣyam* (of Śaṅkara) Vols I and II, Ashtekar Company, Poona, 1927 and 1928.

—, *Minor Works of Śrī Śaṅkarācārya*, Poona, 2nd Ed. 1952.

BHĀMATĪ: See Śaṅkara, *Brahma Sūtra Bhāṣya*.

BHĀRAVI, *Kirātārjunīyam*, ed. with Mallinātha's comm. and Hindi trans., Śobhita Miśra, Banaras, 1952.

BHARTṚHARI, *Vākyapadīya*, complete text ed. K.V. Abhyankar and V.P. Limaye, Poona, 1965.

BHĀSKARA, *Brahma Sūtra Bhāṣya*, Banaras, 1915.

BHATT, G.P., *Epistemology of the Bhāṭṭa School of Pūrva Mīmāmsā*, Varanasi, 1962.

BHATTACHARYA, V.S., *Āgama Śāstra of Gauḍapāda*, Calcutta, 1943, (Abbreviated Ā.Ś.G.).

BIARDEAU, M., *La définition dans la pensée indienne*, J.A., 1957, 371-384.

— , (Contribution on Indian philosophy to) *Encyclopédie de la Pléiade, Histoire de la philosophie*, I, Paris, 1969.

—, *La philosophie de Maṇḍana Miśra*, Paris, 1969.

—, *Quelques réflexions sur l'apophatisme de Śaṅkara*, I.I.J., 1959, 81-100.

—, *Théorie de la connaissance et philosophie de la parole dans le brahmanisme classique*, Paris and the Hague, 1964.

— , *La démonstration du Sphoṭa par Maṇḍana Miśra*, Pondichéry, 1958.

BOETZELAER, J.M. van, *Sureśvara's Taittirīyopaniṣad Bhāṣyavārttika*, Leiden, 1971.

BÖHTLINGK, O., *Sanskrit-Wörterbuch*, 3 vols, St Petersburg, 1879-89, reprinted Graz, 1959.

BUDHAKAR, G.V., '*Is the Advaita of Śaṅkara Buddhism in Disguise?*', Quarterly Journal of the Mythic Society, Bangalore, several parts, *incipit* Vol. XXIV, 1933: 1-18, 160-176, 252-265, 314-326.

BÜHLER, G., (trans.) *Āpastamba Dharma Sūtra*, S.B.E.

BUITENEN, J.A.B. van and DEUTSCH, E., *A Source Book of Advaita Vedānta*, Hawaii, 1971.

CAMMANN, K., *Das System des Advaita nach der Lehre Prakaśātmans*, Wiesbaden, 1965.

CANDRAKĪRTI: see Nāgārjuna.

CHATTERJI, S.K., *Indo-Aryan and Hindi*, 2nd Ed., Calcutta, 1960, reprinted 1969.

CHATTOPADHYAYA, D.P., *History of Indian Philosophy*, New Delhi, 1964.

CINNASWĀMĪ ŚĀSTRĪ (ed.) *Āpastamba Dharma Sūtra*, Banaras,1932.

CITSUKHA, *Abhiprāya Prakāśikā* (Comm. on Maṇḍana's *Brahma Siddhi)*, see Anantakṛṣṇa Śāstrī.

CRESSON, A., *Les courants de la pensée philosophique française*, Vol. 2, Paris, 1927.

CURTIUS, G., *Principles of Greek Etymology*, trans. A.S. Wilkins, London, two vols, 1875 and 1876.

DAKṢIṆĀMŪRTI STOTRA, ed. A. Mahādeva Śāstrī and K. Raṅgācārya with Sureśvara's *Mānasollāsa* and explanatory ṭīkās by Svayamprakāśa and Rāmatīrtha, Mysore Oriental Library Publications, 6, 1895.

DAṆḌIN, *Daśakumāra Carita*, ed. and trans. M.R. Kale, 3rd Ed., Bombay, 1925, reprinted Delhi, 1966.

DARŚANODAYA: see Lakshmīpuram Srīnivāsāchār.

DAS GUPTA, S.N., *History of Indian Philosophy*, Vol. V, Cambridge, 1955.

DE, S.K., *Aspects of Sanskrit Literature*, Calcutta, 1959.

DEUSSEN, P., *Erinnerungen an Indien*, Kiel and Leipzig, 1904.

— , *The Philosophy of the Upanishads*, trans. Geden, 1906, reprinted New York, 1966.

—, *Sechzig Upanishad's des Veda*, Leipzig, 3rd Ed. 1921, reprinted Darmstadt, 1963.

—, *Die Sūtra's des Vedānta*, Leipzig, 1887, reprinted Hildesheim, 1966.

—, *The System of the Vedānta*, Chicago, 1912. Abbreviated D.S.V.

—, and Strauss, O., *Vier Philosophische Texte des Mahābhāratam*, Leipzig, 1906.

DEUTSCH, E., *Advaita Vedānta*, Honolulu, 1969. See also van Buitenen, J.A.B.

DEVARAJA, N.K., *An Introduction to Śaṅkara's Theory of Knowledge*, Delhi, 1962.

DEVASTHALI, G., *Mīmāṃsā*, Vol. I, Bombay, 1959.

—, *Śaṅkara's Indebtedness to Mīmāṃsā*, J.O.I.B., 1951-2, 23-30.

DHARMAKĪRTI, *Pramāṇa Vārttikam*, ed. Dvārikādāsa Śāstrī, Varanasi, 1968. See also Prajñākara Gupta.

DĪGHA NIKĀYA, ed. Rhys Davids and Carpenter, Vol. II, Pali Text Society, London, 1966 (reprint).

DOWSON, J., *A Classical Dictionary of Hindu Mythology*, reprinted London, 1968.

ECKHART, Meister, *Sermons and Treatises*, ed. and trans. M. O'C. Walshe, Vol. II, Watkins, London, 1981.

EDGERTON, F., *Buddhist Hybrid Sanskrit Grammar and Dictionary*, Yale University, 1953, two vols. Reprinted Delhi 1970 and 1972.

FRAUWALLNER, E., *Geschichte der indischen Philosophie*, Vols I and II, Vienna, 1953 and 1956. Abbreviated G.I.P.

—, *Materialien zur ältesten Erkenntnislehre der Karma-mīmāṃsā*, Vienna, 1968.

—, *Die Philosophie des Buddhismus*, Berlin, 1958.

GAIL, A., *Bhakti im Bhāgavata Purāṇa*, Wiesbaden, 1969.

GAMBHĪRĀNANDA, Swāmī (trans.), *Brahma-Sūtra Bhāṣya of Śaṅkarācārya*, Calcutta, 1965.

— (trans.), *Chāndogya Upaniṣad with the Commentary of Śaṅkarācārya*, Calcutta, 1983.

— (trans.), *Eight Upaniṣads with the Commentary of Śaṅkarācārya*, Calcutta, two vols 1957 and 1958. (Vol.I comprises Īśa, Kena, Kaṭha, Taitt: Vol.II, Ait., Muṇḍ., Māṇḍ.with G.K. and Praśna.)

GARBE, R., *Die Sāṅkhya Philosophie*, Leipzig, 1917.

GAUTAMA DHARMA SŪTRA, trans. G. Bühler, S.B.E.

GELDNER, K.F., *Der Rigveda*, Harvard, four vols, 1951-57.

GHATE, V. S., *Le Vedānta*, Paris, 1918.

GLASENAPP, H. von, *Entwicklungsstufen des indischen Denkens*, Halle, 1940.

— , *Die Philosophie der Inder*, Stuttgart, 1949 (abbreviated as '*Einführung*')

— , *Stufenweg zum Göttlichen*, Baden Baden, 1948.

GOKHALE, D.V. see under Texts of Śaṅkara (above), *Bhagavad Gītā Bhāṣya* and *Upadeśa Sāhasrī*..

GONDA, J., *Inleiding tot het Indische Denken*, Antwerp, 1948.

— , *Les religions de l'Inde*, Vols I and II, Paris, 1953 and 1956.

GOPĪNĀTH, see Kavirāj.

GOUGH, A.E. see *Vaiśeṣika Sūtras*.

GOVINDĀNANDA: see Śaṅkara, *Brahma Sūtra Bhāṣya*.

GROUSSET, R., *Les philosophies indiennes*, two vols, Paris, 1931.

HACKER, P. Most of Paul Hacker's important articles on Advaita Vedanta were assembled in *Kleine Schriften* (see below). These can now be read in English translation in *Philology and Confrontation*, ed. and trans. Wilhelm Halbfass, State University of New York Press, 1995.

—, *Eigentümlichkeiten der Lehre und Terminologie Śaṅkaras*, Z.D.M.G., 1950, 246ff. (Halbfass, 57ff).

—, *Die Lehre von den Realitätsgraden im Advaita-Vedānta*, Z.M.R., 1952, 277ff. (Halbfass, 137ff).

—, *Jayanta Bhaṭṭa und Vācaspati Miśra, ihre Zeit und ihre Bedeutung für die Chronologie des Vedānta* included in *Beiträge... Walter Schubring dargebracht* (see Schubring) 160-169.

—, *Kleine Schriften*, herausgegeben von L. Schmithausen, Wiesbaden, 1978.

—, *Prahlāda*, Wiesbaden, 1960.

—, *Śaṅkara der Yogin und Śaṅkara der Advaitin*, W.Z.K.S.O. 1968/1969, 119ff. (Halbfass, 101ff).

—, *Śaṅkarācārya and Śaṅkarabhagavatpāda*, New Indian Antiquary, April-June 1947. Preferably consulted in the corrected version in *Kleine Schriften*, 41ff. (Halbfass, 41ff).

—, *Untersuchungen über Texte des frühen Advaita Vāda*, I, Wiesbaden, 1951. (abbreviated 'Texte').

—, *Upadeshasāhasrī, Gadyaprabandha* (Prose Section) übersezt und erläutert, Bonn, 1949.

—, *Vedānta Studien* I, Die Welt des Orients, Wuppertal, 1948, 240.

—, *Vivarta*, Wiesbaden, 1953.

HALBFASS, W. (ed. and trans.), *Philology and Confrontation*, State University of New York Press, 1995. (See above, under Hacker)

HAUER, J.W., *Der Yoga*, Stuttgart, 1958.

HAZRA, R.C., *Studies in the Purāṇic Records*, Dacca, 1940.

HEIMANN, B., *Studien zur Eigenart indischen Denkens*, Tübingen, 1930.

HIRIYANNA, M., *Essentials of Indian Philosophy*, London, 1949.

—, *Outlines of Indian Philosophy*, London, 1932.

HUME, R.E., *The Thirteen Principal Upanishads*, 2nd Edition of 1931, reprinted Madras (O.U.P.), 1958.

INGALLS, Daniel H.H., *Śaṅkara on the Question 'Whose is Avidyā?'* in P.E.W. 1953, 68ff.

— , *Śaṅkara's Arguments against the Buddhists*, in P.E.W., 1954, 291-316.

ĪŚVARA KṚṢṆA, *Sāṅkhya Kārikās* with *Tattvakaumudi* Commentary of Vācaspati Miśra, text and trans. Gaṅgānātha Jhā, ed. H.D. Sharma, Poona, 1934.

IYER, K.A. Subramania, *Bhartṛhari*, Poona, 1969.

JACOB, Col. G.A., *A Handful of Popular Maxims*, in three Parts, Bombay, 1900, 1902 and 1904.

— , *A Concordance to the Principal Upanishads and Bhagavad Gītā*, 1891, re-issued Delhi, 1963.

— see also under Sadānanda and Sureśvara.

JAGADĀNANDA, Svāmī, *A Thousand Teachings* (the *Upadeśa Sāhasrī* of Śaṅkara), text and trans., Madras, 2nd Ed. 1949.

JAIMINI: see under Śabara.

JASPERS, K., *The Way to Wisdom*, London, 1951.

JAYA DEVA, *Gītagovinda Kāvyam*, ed. Nārāyaṇa Rāma Ācārya, Bombay, 9th Ed., 1949.

JHĀ, Gaṅgānātha, *Pūrva Mīmāṃsā in its Sources*, Banaras, 1942.

— , *Chāndogya Upanishad and Śrī Śaṅkara's Commentary* (2 volumes), Madras, 1899

— see also under Īśvara Kṛṣṇa, Kumārila Bhaṭṭa, Śabara, Praśastapāda.

JHALAKĪKARA, B.J., *Nyāya Kośa*, Bombay, 3rd Ed., 1928.

JOHNSTON, E.H., *Early Sāṅkhya*, London, 1937.

JOSHI, L.M., *Studies in the Buddhistic Culture of India*, Delhi, 1967.

JOŚĪ, T.L. (= Jośi, Tarkatīrtha Lakṣmaṇaśāstrī), *Vaidika Saṃskṛti kā Vikāsa* (Hindi trans. from the Marathi), Bombay, 1957.

— , *Dharma Kośa Upaniṣat Kāṇḍa*, Wai (Maharashtra), 1950.

KAṆĀDA: see Vaiśeṣika Sūtras.

KAVIRĀJ, Gopīnāth, *Bhūmikā* (Introduction to Acyuta Grantha Mālā Ed. of Śaṅkara's B.S.Bh.), Banaras, 1937.

KEITH, A.B. (ed. and trans.), *Aitareya Āraṇyaka*, Oxford, 1909.

—, *A History of Sanskrit Literature*, Oxford, 1920.

—, *The Karma-Mīmāṃsā*, Calcutta, 1921.

—, *The Sāṃkhya System*, Calcutta, 1924.

—, (trans.) *Taittirīya Saṃhitā*, Harvard Oriental Series, 2 vols, 1914.

KṚṢṆA MIŚRA (ed. and trans.), *Prabodha Candrodaya*, Sita Krishna Nambiar, Delhi, 1971.

KṚṢṆA YAJVAN, *Mīmāṃsā-Paribhāṣā*, text and trans. Mādhavānanda, Calcutta, 1948.

KULLŪKA: see under Manu Smṛti.

KUMĀRILA BHAṬṬA, *Mīmāṃsā Śloka Vārttika* (abbreviated Ś.V.), Banaras, 1898-1899; trans. Gaṅgānātha Jhā, Calcutta, 1900-1908.

—, *Tantra Vārttika*, ed. Gangādhara Shāstrī, Benares, 1882-1903; trans. Gaṅgānātha Jhā, Bibliotheca Indica, Calcutta, 1903-24.

KUNJUNNI RAJA, K., *The Date of Śaṅkarācārya and Allied Problems*, Brahma Vidyā (= Adyar Library Bulletin) Vol. 24, 1960, 125-48.

—, *Indian Theories of Meaning*, Adyar, Madras, 1963.

KŪRMA PURĀṆA, Bombay, 1927.

LACOMBE, O., *L'Absolu selon le Védanta*, Paris, 1937.

LAKSHMĪPURAM SRĪNIVĀSĀCHĀR, *Darśanodaya*, Mysore, 1933.

LEGGETT, T., *The Chapter of the Self* (translation and exposition of Śaṅkara's *Vivaraṇa* on Praśna I, Paṭala 8 of *Āpastamba Dharma Sūtra)*, London, 1978.

LEHMANN, A., *Aberglaube und Zauberei*, 3rd Ger. Ed., Stuttgart, 1925.

MĀDHAVĀNANDA, SVĀMĪ (trans.), *The Bṛhadāraṇyaka Upanishad with the Commentary of Śaṅkarācārya*, Calcutta, 6th Ed., 1985.

MADHUSŪDANA, see Sarvajña Muni.

MĀGHA, *Śiśupālavadham*, Chowkamba Vidyā Bhavan, Banaras,1955.

MAHĀBHĀRATA: G.P. Ed. (Mūlamātra). Also consulted, critical Ed. of V.S. Sukthankar, Poona, 1933-72. See also Deussen and Strauss.

MAHADEVAN, T.M.P., *Gauḍapāda*, Madras, 1952.

—, (ed.) *Word Index to the Brahma-Sūtra Bhāṣya of Śaṅkara*, Madras, two Parts, 1971 and 1973.

MAHĀNĀRAYAṆA UPANISHAD, ed. and trans. J. Varenne, Paris, 1960.

MAṆḌANA MIŚRA, *Brahma Siddhi* (abbreviated B.Sid.), ed. Kuppuswami Shastri, Madras, 1937. See also Anantakṛṣna Śāstrī, Biardeau, Schmithausen and Vetter.

MANU SMṚTI, with Comm. of Kullūka, Bombay, 1902.

MATICS, Marion L., *Entering the Path of Enlightenment*, trans. of *Bodhicaryāvatāraḥ*, London, 1970. See also Śānti Deva.

MAYEDA, S., *The Authenticity of the Upadeśa Sāhasrī*, J.A.O.S., 1965, No.2, 178-196.

— , *On the Authenticity of the Māṇḍūkya and the Gauḍapādīya Bhāṣya*, Brahma Vidyā (= Adyar Library Bulletin), 1967-8, 74ff.

— , *On Śaṅkara's Authorship of the Kenopaniṣadbhāṣya*, I.I.J., X (1967), 33-35.

—, *The Authenticity of the Bhagavadgītābhāṣya ascribed to Śaṅkara*, W.Z.K.S.O. IX (1965), 155-197.

— , *Śaṅkara's Upadeśa Sāhasrī*, critically edited with Introduction and Indices, Tokyo, 1973.

— , *A Thousand Teachings, The Upadeśasāhasrī of Śaṅkara*, trans. with Introduction and notes, Tokyo, 1979.

MONIER-WILLIAMS, Sir M., *Sanskrit-English Dictionary*, Oxford, 2nd Ed., 1899.

MORICHINI, G., *Early Vedānta Philosophy* (being a short summary of H. Nakamura's work on that subject) in the periodical *East and West* (Rome), 1960, 33-39.

MÜLLER, Max, *Sacred Books of the East* (abbreviated S.B.E.), Vol. XV, Oxford, 1884. Reprinted Delhi.

MURTI, T.R.V., *The Central Philosophy of Buddhism* (abbreviated C.P.B.), London, 1955.

— , *The Two Definitions of Brahman in the Advaita*, in *Krishna Chandra Bhattacharya Memorial Volume*, Almaner, 1958, 135-150.

MUS, P., *Barabadur*, Hanoi, 1935.

NĀGĀRJUNA, *Mūlamādhyamika Kārikās*, ed. with *Prasannapadā* Commentary of Candrakīrti by de La Vallée Poussin, St. Petersburg, 1903-1913.

NAKAMURA, H., *A History of Early Vedanta Philosophy*, Part One, New Delhi, 1983.

— , *The Vedānta Philosophy as was Revealed in Buddhist Scriptures*, in Dr. Maṇḍan Miśra (ed.), *Pañcāmṛtam,*Delhi, 1968, pp 1-74.

—, *Vedanta Tetsugaku No Hatten (Development of Vedānta Philosophy)*, in *Indian Philosophical Thought, Vol. III*, Tokyo, 1955.

— see also Morichini, G.

NARENDRADEVA, *Bauddha-Dharma-Darśana*, Patna, 1956.

NIKHILĀNANDA, *The Māṇḍūkyopaniṣad with Gauḍapāda's Kārikā and Śaṅkara's Commentary*, Calcutta, 4th ed., 1955.

OLDENBERG, H., *Die Lehre der Upanishaden und die Anfänge des Buddhismus*, Göttingen, 1923.

— , *Die Weltanschauung der Brāhmaṇa-Texte*, Göttingen, 1919.

ÖPIK, E.J., *The Oscillating Universe*, Mentor Books, N.Y., 1960.

OTTO, R., *Mysticism East and West*, N.Y., 1932.

PADMAPĀDA, see PAÑCAPĀDIKĀ

PADOUX, A., *Recherches sur la symbolique et l'énergie de la parole dans certains textes Tantriques*, Paris, 1964.

PAÑCAPĀDIKĀ (abbreviated P.P.), a work attributed to Padmapāda, ed. S. Shrīrāma Shāstrī and S.R. Krishnamūrthi Shāstrī, Madras, 1958. For trans. see Venkataramiah.

PANDEY, S.L., *Pre-Śaṅkara Advaita Philosophy*, Allahabad, 1974.

PĀṆINI, *The Ashṭādhyāyī of Pāṇini*, ed. and trans. S.C. Vasu, two vols, 1891, reprinted Delhi, 1962.

PARAMĀRTHA SĀRA: ed. with the *Vivaraṇa* of Rāghavānanda by S. N. Śukla, Banaras, 1933. For trans., see S.S. Śāstrī, below.

PASSMORE, J., *A Hundred Years of Philosophy*, Pelican Books, Harmondsworth, 1968.

PATAÑJALI, *Yoga Sūtras* with Comms. of Vyāsa and Vācaspati, Bombay, 1892.

—, (trans.) J.H. Woods, Harvard, 1914, reprinted Delhi, 1972.

— : see also Śaṅkara for (attributed) *Vivaraṇa* on Vyāsa's Comm. (Bhāṣya) to *Yoga Sūtras*.

POTTER, Karl, *Bibliography of Indian Philosophies*, Delhi, 1970.

PRAJÑĀKARA GUPTA, *Pramāṇa Vārtika Bhāṣyam*, ed. Rāhula Sāṃkṛtyāyana, Patna, 1953.

PRAKĀŚĀTMAN, *Vivaraṇa*, ed. S. Shrīrāma Shāstrī and S.R. Krishnamūrthi Shāstrī, Madras, 1958. See also Cammann, above.

PRAŚASTAPĀDA, *Praśastapāda-Bhāṣya* (or *Padārthadharma Saṅgraha*), with *Nyāyakandalī* of Shrī Dhara, Banaras, 1895. Eng. trans. Gaṅgānath Jhā, Banaras, 1916.

PŪRVA MĪMĀṂSĀ SŪTRAS: see under Śabara.

RADHAKRISHNAN, Sir S., *Indian Philosophy*, London, two vols, 1927.

—, *The Principal Upanishads*, London, 1953.

RĀGHORĀM, B. Shivprasād: (Publisher) *Hundred and Eight Upanishads*, Banaras, 1938 (Sanskrit text only).

RĀMA DEVA: see Jaiminīya Upanishad Brāhmaṇa.

RĀMĀNUJA, *Śrī Bhāṣya*, ed. Vāsudeva Śāstrī Abhyaṅkar, Bombay, 1914.

RATNAPRABHĀ: see Śaṅkara, *Brahma Sūtra Bhāṣya*.

RENOU, L., *Grammaire et Védanta*, in J.A., 1957, 121-132.

RENOU and FILLIOZAT, *L'Inde Classique*, two vols, Paris and Hanoi, 1947 and 1953.

ṚG VEDA, Rig Veda (Abbreviated R.V.): see also Geldner.

— , *Ṛg Veda Saṃhitā*, with Comm. of Sāyana, Vedic Research Institute, Poona, 5 vols 1933-51.

RITTER, H., *Das Meer der Seele*, Leiden, 1955.

RŪMĪ, Jalālu'ddīn, *Mathnawī*, trans. R.A. Nicholson, London, Vol.I, 1926.

RÜPING, K., *Studien zur Frühgeschichte der Vedānta Philosophie*, Wiesbaden, 1977.

ŚABARA, Jaimini's *Pūrva Mīmāṃsā Sūtra Bhāṣya*, Calcutta, two vols, 1873 and 1887. Trans. Gaṅgānātha Jhā, G.O.S., 3 vols, 1933, 1934 and 1936. See also Frauwallner.

SACCIDĀNANDENDRA SVĀMIN (abbreviated as Sac.) All Sac's works are published by the Adhyātma Prakāśa Kāryālaya, Holenarsipur, Karnataka, India, unless otherwise stated.

—, *Brahmavidyā Rahasya Vivṛtiḥ*, 1969.

—, *Gītā-Śāstrārtha-Vivekaḥ*, 1965.

—, *Intuition of Reality*, 1973.

— , *Īśāvāsya Upaniṣad* with Śaṅkara's Bhāṣya and author's Sanskrit *ṭīkā* (written under the lay name of Y. Subrahmanya Śarmā), 1937.

—, *Māṇḍūkya Rahasya Vivṛtiḥ*, 1958. (abbreviated M.R.V.)

— , *The Method of the Vedanta* (abbreviated M.V.), London, 1989 (Translation by A.J. Alston of *Vedānta Prakriyā Pratyabhijñā*, q.v.).

—, *Misconceptions about Śaṅkara*, 1973.

—, *Śaṅkara's Clarification of certain Vedantic Concepts*, 1969.

— , *Śuddha-Śaṅkara-Prakriyā-Bhāskara* (abbreviated Ś.Ś.P.B.), quoted from Sanskrit Ed. in 3 parts, 1964. Available in English, 3 parts 1965-1968, subtitled *Light on the Vedantic Method according to Śaṅkara*.

—, *Sugamā* (Sanskrit exposition of Śaṅkara's Adhyāsa-bhāṣya), 1955.

—, *Taittirīya Upanishad Shikshāvallī,* ed. with Shaṅkara's Commentary and editor's Sanskrit notes, 1961.

—, *Taittirīya Upanishad Ānandavallī-Bhṛguvallī,* ed. with Shaṅkara's Commentary and editor's *Bhāṣyārtha Vimarśinī* sub-commentary, 1962.

—, *Vedānta Prakriyā Pratyabhijñā*, 1964. For an English translation of this work, see *The Method of the Vedānta*, previous page.

—, *Viśuddha Vedānta Sāra*, 1968. (Abbreviated V.V.S.)

SADĀNANDA, *Vedānta Sāra*, ed. with two commentaries, Col. G.A. Jacob, 5th revised Ed., 1934.

— , text of *Vedānta Sāra* with Eng. trans. Nikhilānanda Svāmin, Calcutta, 1947.

SADĀNANDA YATI, *Advaita Brahma Siddhi*, Calcutta, 1888-90.

ṢAḌVIṂŚA BRĀHMAṆA, ed. K. Klemm, Gütersloh, 1894. Trans. W.B. Bollée, Utrecht, 1956.

SAHASRABUDDHE, M.T., *A Survey of Pre-Śaṅkara Advaita Vedānta*, Poona, 1968.

SĀṄKṚTYĀYANA, Rāhula, *Darśana Dig-Darśana*, Allahabad, 2nd Ed., 1947. (Hindi).

ŚĀNTI DEVA, *Bodhicaryāvatāraḥ*, ed. P.L.Vaidya, Darbhanga, 1960. See also M.L. Matics.

SARVAJÑA MUNI, *Saṅkṣepa Śārīrakam* with the Commentary of Madhusūdana, Banaras, 1924.

Sarvajñātman and Sarvajñātma Muni: alternative forms of the above name.

ŚĀSTRĪ: sometimes interchanged with Shāstrī, q.v.

ŚĀSTRĪ, A. Mahādeva, *The Bhagavad-Gītā with the Commentary of Śaṅkarācārya*, Madras, 1897. Reprinted, Madras, 1977.

— , *Dakshiṇāmūrti Stotra of Śrī Śaṅkarāchārya*, Madras, 3rd Ed., 1978. Contains Sanskrit text and Eng. trans. of the *Mānasollāsa Vārttika* attributed to Sureśvara. See also entry under *Dakṣiṇāmūrti*

Stotra above for Sanskrit edition of text and commentaries.

ŚĀSTRĪ, Maṅgaladeva, *Bhāratīya Saṃskṛti kā Vikāsa*, Part II, *Aupaniṣada Dhārā*, Banaras, 1966 (Hindi).

ŚĀSTRĪ, Rāmānanda Tivārī, *Śrī Śaṃkarācārya kā ācāra darśana*, Allahabad, 1950 (Hindi).

ŚĀSTRĪ, S.S. Sūryanārāyaṇa, *The Paramārtha Sāra of Ādi Śeṣa*, Bombay, 1941.

— and C.K. Rājā, *The Bhāmatī: Catussūtrī*, Adyar, Madras, 1933.

ŚATAPATHA BRĀHMAṆA, trans. Eggeling, S.B.E. (in 5 parts).

SCHMITHAUSEN, L., *Maṇḍana Miśras Vibhrama Vivekaḥ*, Vienna, 1965.

SCHUBRING, W. (Festschrift) *Beiträge zur indischen Philologie... Walther Schubring dargebracht*, Hamburg, 1951.

SHARMA, L.N., *Kashmir Śaivism*, Banaras, 1972.

SHĀSTRĪ : sometimes interchanged with Śāstrī, q.v.

SHASTRI, Hari Prasad: see Vālmīki and Vidyāraṇya.

SILBURN, L., *Instant et Cause*, Paris, 1955.

SOGEN, Yamakami, *Systems of Buddhistic Thought*, Calcutta, 1912.

ŚRĪ HARṢA, *Śrī Harṣa's Plays*, ed. and trans. Bak Kun Bae, Bombay, 1964.

SRĪNIVĀSĀCHARĪ, P.N., *The Philosophy of Bhedābheda*, Madras, 1934.

STAAL, J.F., *Advaita and Neoplatonism*, Madras, 1961.

STCHERBATSKY, Th., *The Conception of Buddhist Nirvāṇa*, revised and enlarged edition by Jaidev Singh, Bhāratīya Vidyā Prakāśana Edition, Banaras, n.d.

—, *Buddhist Logic*, Vol. II, Leningrad, 1930.

—, *Central Conception of Buddhism*, London, 1923.

—, *La théorie de la connaissance et la logique chez les Bouddhistes tardifs*, Paris, 1926.

STRAUSS, O., *Indische Philosophie*, Munich, 1925. See also Deussen.

SŪRA DĀSA, *Sūra Sāgara*, ed. Vājapeyī, Vārāṇasī, 2 vols, 1953 and 1956.

SUREŚVARA, *Bṛhadāraṇyaka Bhāṣya Vārttikam* (abbreviated B.B.V.) ed. with Ānandagiri's ṭīkā in the Ā.S.S. Ed., three vols, Poona, 1892-1894. See also Ānandapūrṇa.

—, (Attributed) *Mānosollāsa*. Commentary on *Dakṣiṇāmūrti Stotra*, q.v.

— , *Naiṣkarmya Siddhi* (abbreviated N.Sid.), ed. with Jñānottama's Commentary, by Col. G.A. Jacob and revised by M. Hiriyanna, Bombay,1925. Trans. by A.J. Alston as *The Realization of the Absolute*, Shanti Sadan, 2nd Ed. 1971.

— , (Attributed) *Pañcīkaraṇa Vārttika* in *Panchīkaraṇam of Shree Shankarāchārya*, Edited with six commentaries, Gujarati Printing Press, Bombay, 1930.

—, *The Sambandha Vārttika*, text and Eng. trans. T.M.P. Mahadevan, Madras, 1958.

—, *Taittirīya Bhāṣya Vārttika* (abbreviated T.B.V.), Ā.S.S. Ed. with ṭīkā of Ānandagiri, 1911. For Eng. trans. see Boetzelaer, above.

TAITTIRĪYA ĀRAṆYAKA, Ā.S.S., Poona, Vol. I, 1926.

TAITTIRĪYA BRĀHMAṆA, ed. Rājendralāl Mitra, Calcutta, 1870.

TAITTTIRĪYA SAṂHITĀ: see Keith, above.

THIBAUT, G., *The Vedānta Sūtras with the Commentary of Śaṅkarācārya* (= Brahma Sūtra Bhāṣya, B.S.Bh.), Eng. trans., Parts I and II.

TROṬAKA (or Toṭaka), *Śruti Sāra Samuddharaṇa*, ed. Kevalānanda Svāmin, Ā.S.S. Ed., Poona, 1936.

UDDYOTAKARA, *Nyāya Vārttikam*, ed. Dvivedin and Dravid, Benares, 1916-7.

UI, Hakuju, *Vaiśeṣika Philosophy according to the Daśapadārthaśāstra*, Chinese Text with English translation and notes, Banaras, 1962.

UPĀDHYĀYA, Baladeva, *Śrī Śaṃkarācārya*, Allahabad, 1950. (Hindi).

—, *Śrī-Śaṃkara-Dig-Vijaya*, Sanskrit text with Hindi trans., Hardwar, 1944.

UPĀDHYĀYA, B.S., *Bauddha Darśana tathā anya Bhāratīya Darśana*, 2 vols, Calcutta, 1954 (Hindi).

UPĀDHYĀYA, Rāmajī, *Bhārata kī Saṃskṛti-Sādhanā*, Allahabad, 1967. (Hindi).

VĀCASPATI MIŚRA: see under Texts of Śaṅkara, *Brahma Sūtra Bhāṣya, Bhāmatī sub-commentary*. See also Īśvara Kṛṣṇa.

VAIŚEṢIKA SŪTRAS, with Comm. of Śaṅkara Miśra, ed. and trans. A.E. Gough, Benares, 1873, reprinted New Delhi, 1975.

—, ed. Jīvānanda, Calcutta, 1886.

VALLABHĀCĀRYA, *Aṇu Bhāṣya*, text and *Bālabodhinī* commentary, two vols, Bombay, 1921 and 1926.

VĀLMĪKI, *The Ramayana of Valmiki* (trans. H.P. Shastri), three vols., London, 2nd revised Ed. of Vol. I, 1962.

VĀSIṢṬHA *Dharma Sūtra*, trans. G. Bühler, S.B.E.

VĀTSYĀYANA, *Nyāya Sūtra Bhāṣya*, Poona, 1939. Eng. trans. Gaṅgānāth Jhā, Poona, 1939.

VENKAṬANĀTHA, *Tattva Muktā Kalāpaḥ* with *Sarvārtha Siddhi* and *Bhāva Prakāśa*, Mysore, Vol. II., 1940.

VENKATARAMIAH, D., *The Pañcapādikā of Padmapāda*, G.O.S., Baroda, 1948.

— , *Aitareyopaniṣad with Śaṅkarācārya's Bhāṣya*, text and Eng. trans., Bangalore, 1934.

VETTER, T., *Maṇḍana Miśra's Brahmasiddhiḥ, Brahmakāṇḍaḥ* only, annotated German trans., Vienna, 1969.

— , *Zur Bedeutung des Illusionismus bei Śaṅkara*, W.Z.K.S.O. 1968/69, 407-423.

—, *Erkenntnisprobleme bei Dharmakīrti*, Vienna, 1964.

VIDYĀRAṆYA, *Bṛhadāraṇyaka Bhāṣya Vārttika Sāra* (B.B.V.S.), Acyuta Grantha Mālā Ed., Banaras, two vols, 1941 and 1943.

— , *Panchadashi* (= Pañcadaśī, abbreviated P.D.), text and trans. by H.P. Shastri, 2nd revised Ed., London, 1965.

VIJÑĀNA BHIKṢU, *Sāṃkhya Pravacana Bhāṣya*, ed. R. Garbe, Cambridge, Mass., 1895.

VIMUKTĀTMAN, *Iṣṭa-Siddhi*, ed. Hiriyanna, G.O.S., Baroda, 1933.

VIṢṆU PURĀṆA: G.P. Ed. with the Hindi trans. of Śrī Munilāla Gupta, 1937.

VIVARAṆA: see Prakaśātman.

VYĀSA: see Patañjali.

WARDER, A.K., *Outlines of Indian Philosophy*, New Delhi, 1971.

WOODS, J.H: see Patañjali.

YĀJÑAVALKYA SMṚTI, with Mitākṣarā Commentary and Hindi trans., Umesh Chandra Pandey, Banaras, 1967.

YAMAKAMI, S: see under Sogen, Y.

YĀSKA, *Nirukti*, Calcutta, 4 vols, 1882-91.

YOGA VĀSIṢṬHA, with the Commentary of Ānandabodhendra, two vols, Bombay, 1937.

YOGA SŪTRAS: see Patañjali.

YUKTI DĪPIKĀ, ed. Ram Chandra Pandeya, Banaras-Delhi, 1967.

The Śaṅkara Source-Book

A Conspectus of the Contents of the Six Volumes

Volume I — Śaṅkara on the Absolute

I. SOURCES OF ŚAṄKARA'S DOCTRINE: HIS LIFE & WORKS

1. A Doctrine of Transcendence
2. Vedas: Saṃhitās, Brāhmaṇas, Upanishads
3. The Smṛti: Viṣṇu worship and Śiva worship
4. The Bhagavad Gītā
5. The Brahma-Sūtras and their Background: Bhartṛprapañca
6. The True Tradition: Gauḍapāda, Draviḍa, Brahmanandin, Sundara Pāṇḍya
7. Doctrine of Illusion before Śaṅkara: Māyā Vāda and Avidyā Vāda
8. Śaṅkara's Date, Life and Works
9. Śaṅkara's School

II. THE DOCTRINE OF NESCIENCE

1. The Nature and Results of Nescience
2. Nescience as Non-Comprehension and False Comprehension
3. The Self and the Not-Self: Non-Discrimination and Mutual Superimposition
4. The Standpoint of Nescience and the Standpoint of Knowledge

III. KNOWLEDGE OF THE ABSOLUTE

1. The Absolute is already known in a general way
2. The Absolute is not known as an object
3. The Path of Negation
4. Going beyond the Mind

IV. THE ABSOLUTE AS BEING, CONSCIOUSNESS AND BLISS

1. The Definition of the Absolute as 'Reality, Knowledge, Infinity'
2. The Absolute as the Self-Existent Principle
3. The Absolute as the Self-Luminous Principle
4. The Absolute as Bliss

Volume II — Śaṅkara on the Creation

V. THE ABSOLUTE AS CREATOR AND CONTROLLER

1. The Absolute as Creator and Controller of the World
2. The Absolute as the Lord
3. The Absolute as the Material and Efficient Cause of the World
4. The Absolute as Inner Ruler
5. The Absolute as the Lord of Māyā

VI. THE WORLD AND ITS PRESIDING DEITIES

1. Sat-kārya Vāda
2. Name and Form: Indeterminability
3. World-periods and Theory of the Elements
4. The Presiding Deities

VII. THE ACOSMIC VIEW

1. The Creation-texts as a Device to teach Non-Duality
2. Nothing can come into being
3. The Argument from Dream

Volume III — Śaṅkara on the Soul

VIII. THE SOUL AND ITS ORGANS AND BODIES

1. The Soul as the Self viewed under External Adjuncts
2. The Organs and Bodies of the Soul
3. The Light that illumines the Soul
4. The Soul and the Lord are not distinct

IX. THE 'STATES' OF THE SOUL AND THEIR TRANSCENDENCE

1. Dream
2. Dreamless Sleep
3. Turīya

Volume IV — Śaṅkara on Rival Views

X. REFUTATION OF INADEQUATE BRAHMINICAL DOCTRINES

1. Refutation of Liberation through Action
2. Refutation of Liberation through Knowledge and Action Conjoined
3. Refutation of Bhedābheda Vāda
4. Refutation of the Pāśupatas and Pāñcarātras
5. Refutation of Sphoṭa Vāda

XI. REFUTATION OF NON-VEDIC WORLD-VIEWS

1. Dialectic (tarka): its Purpose and Rules
2. Refutation of Materialism
3. Refutation of the Sāṅkhyas
4. Refutation of the Vaiśeṣikas
5. Refutation of the Buddhist Schools
6. Refutation of the Jainas

Volume V — Śaṅkara on Discipleship

XII. ADOPTING THE PATH

1. The Wheel of Transmigration
2. The Injunction to Adopt the Path
3. Preliminary Qualifications for the Path
4. Spiritual Qualities to be cultivated on the Path

XIII. THE VEDA AND THE TEACHER

1. The Self can only be known through the Veda
2. The Veda, the Smṛti and Reason
3. The Approach to the Teacher
4. The Teacher and the Texts

Volume VI — Śaṅkara on Enlightenment

XIV. THE INDIRECT PATH

1. Meditation in the Context of the Vedic Ritual (upāsanā)
2. Realization of Identity with Hiraṇyagarbha
3. The Path of the Flame
4. Supernormal Powers on the Indirect Path

XV. THE DIRECT PATH

1. Adhyātma Yoga
2. Devotion (bhakti)
3. Communication of 'That Thou Art'
4. Meditation (dhyāna) and Repeated Affirmation (abhyāsa)
5. Meditation on OM

XVI. THE ENLIGHTENED MAN

1. Enlightenment is not a change of state